CHRISTOPHER BROWNE

89 Fulwell Park Avenue
Twickenham Middlesex TW2 5HG
T: 020 8894 1598 M: 07939 110842
cbrowne@brownemedia.co.uk
www.christopherbrowne.co.uk

18 September 2018

Dear Matt

Here's the incriminating evidence.

Best

The Prying Game

The Prying Game

CHRISTOPHER BROWNE

 Robson Books

First published in Great Britain in 1996 by Robson Books Ltd, Bolsover House, 5–6 Clipstone Street, London W1P 8LE

Copyright © 1996 Christopher Browne

The right of Christopher Browne to be identified as author of this work has been asserted by him in accordance with the Copyright, Designs and Patents Act 1988

British Library Cataloguing in Publication Data
A catalogue record for this title is available from the British Library

ISBN 0 86051 927 9

Photoset in Sabon by Derek Doyle & Associates, Mold, Clwyd. Printed and bound in Great Britain by WBC Book Manufacturers Ltd, Bridgend, Mid-Glamorgan.

Contents

Introduction

Britain is a nation of eavesdroppers. Every day a new scandal, indiscretion or lapse of honour is inflicted on us, sending us into agonies of expectation about who did what to whom and how often. Yet we are usually the unwilling party in these rituals. The sad fact is we have become ciphers of the daily news media, the reluctant participants in an orgy of self-destruction and make-believe. Instead of relaying events to us in a calm and reasoned manner, with clearly though-out ideas, opinions and arguments, the news media disgorges a barrage of sleaze and sensation that often has little bearing on truth or reality. We have become innocent pawns in a daily misinformation factory, forced to look on helplessly at a world of government cover-ups, frolicsome politicians, heroine-addicted pop-stars, bogus charities and crooked companies.

It is a situation from which there is no escape. The British news media is a power unto itself, one moment exposing society's frailties and hypocrisies, the next creating bogus superstars, flawed public figures, deceitful governments and corrupt captains of industry. The media has even assumed the role of Britain's second government opposition, cajoling ministers, politicians and leaders and influencing decisions in the House of Commons, sometimes more aggressively than Her Majesty's official Opposition.

Social commentator, moral guardian, wise counsellor? Hardly. Today's news media is often little less than a relentless predator, projecting itself as Britain's irreverent spokesman on everything popular, outrageous, traditional or offbeat; the fickle judge of our wrong-doings; the preserver of our eccentricities; the creator of our habits and the pioneer of our follies.

One by one, it has undermined the institutions we once held dear. Church, establishment, royal family and State, all have been ridiculed with ritualistic glee, leaving us with little more to cherish than our families and friends and a society in which it is trendy to make cheap jibes about our fellow men and to snipe about the state of a shallow and anxious nation.

The Prying Game asks whether we can prevent the news media from taking complete control of our lives and becoming Britain's first Big Brother. Or have we left it too late?

1

The Power Game

'Journalism: a profession whose business is to explain to others what it personally does not understand.'

Lord Northcliffe

Vanity is the key to success in journalism. Vanity and the actor's ability to show off. The most versatile journalists have invincible egos, giving them the courage to write or talk about any given subject without fear of reproach and the confidence to bedazzle an audience on paper or live on radio or television. Many journalists are cynical. It is a form of protection against the unending flow of violence, crime, catastrophe and human impropriety that pours into the average newsroom each day. Yet these cynics are often humorous, witty, charming and companionable people, social animals who need to shine in a hectic world of glamour, make-believe and hard living.

Working in the news media is similar to the struggle to survive in a ghetto, a writers' ghetto in which decisions are made at random, personal niceties ignored in the pursuit of the story, and the ultimate goal is the first edition. It is a ghetto in which those with the right blend of talent, determination and cunning shine and those with ambition and the will to succeed reach the top. It is, in short, a power game where each man is out for himself and where, as in all competitive networks, cliques and old boy networks thrive. It could be a group who have worked together in a national newspaper office in Manchester (the northern equivalent of Fleet Street); radio sub-editors who drink together in the same pub or a group of television reporters who share similar interests – even if the main one is the toppling of the producer!

The news media is a small, rarefied breed with immense power and influence. The former *Daily Telegraph* editor, Lord Deedes, said: 'There is a great invisible struggle going on as to who really has the most power – the Government or the newspapers.' To which can safely be added radio and television. Government has the last word, but the news media has the influence to change events and cause considerable damage if it so wishes – and its clout continues to increase. As the American writer James Fenimore Cooper put it: 'If newspapers are useful in overthrowing tyrants, it is only to establish a tyranny of their own.'

The British news media has reached a stage where it both reports on and creates trends. If a newspaper pompously announces that an indiscretion by a member of the royal family is a constitutional issue, it immediately becomes one, and for days our eyes and ears are assailed by the rights and wrongs of royal behaviour. Yet, in spite of its power, the news media has a short memory. An issue that is red-hot one day will disappear the next – even if we were told in the first breathless reports that it was a matter of great national importance.

Like a puppet-master, the media dangles its ideas tantalizingly in front of its audience and then whips them away again. If the media tells a plausible story about the Isle of Wight applying for and being rejected as a member of the European Union, we are as likely as not to believe it, particularly if the story is backed up by quotes from influential sources. Then we might chance to discover that oranges are being used for research into flu vaccines or that giraffes are originally descended from ostriches. Or else there is the classic speculative story such as sightings of pumas on Bodmin Moor, Cornwall, or the Surrey Puma which has been 'spotted' in the woods behind Purley railway station every year since 1963.

Another media favourite is the Unidentified Flying Object, sightings of which are chronicled in great depth by experts, psychics and scientists and supported by several thousand blurred images on camera. These stories often read like extracts from a science fiction novel. Is the UFO about to land and visit its common enemy – Man? Is it carrying a party of little green men from Mars on a daily excursion? Is it part of a spying mission making plans for an attack or is it the leader of an inter-planetary reconnaissance force inspecting its cosmic neighbours? And what are those blurred little matchstick images? Are they the Martians themselves trying out their new surroundings? The speculation is endless. We just have to keep on guessing. Seeing a UFO story in print, and not as part of the excited ramblings of a regular in the local saloon bar, makes it all the more convincing, though it may turn out to be a hoax dreamed up by an eccentric prankster.

Whatever the story, if the evidence is well presented and the facts apparently documented, who are we to argue with its authenticity? Quite simply, the news media is able to use its powers of creativity to manipulate the public.

And who is to say what is news and what is not? Perhaps there is a secret network that issues 56,000 items each year from a secret word processor in Bulgaria and regurgitates them around the world? Sometimes it is difficult to tell fact from fiction. How can we be sure that last night's news bulletin about an early general election is not the product of the fevered imagination of a No 10 Downing Street press officer or an announcement that thousands have been killed in a Somalian uprising is not a piece of United Nations propaganda?

Why are some items like the Bosnian war highlighted for weeks on end and then suddenly dropped from our newspapers and television screens for several more, before reappearing for another popular run? Is it because discussing foreign policy is subject to intellectual fads and fashions or, perhaps, a convenient way for an editor to justify the high resources his newspaper or programme spends on overseas correspondents? Or are there other, more sinister, forces at work such as government pressure, the proprietor's trading interests or perhaps a clandestine telephone call from the CIA or MI6.

Alternatively, the reason may be entirely genuine. The war may have temporary flare-ups and cessation periods and the media is merely reacting to these as and when they occur. The problem is that much of today's news is sold to us purely on the whims of the media itself. In a country that advocates the freedom of the press, we are rarely told the reasons for news coverage – except for the occasional investigative article or programme in which the media decides to make its own candid revelations.

News is transient and the British public likes variety in its bulletins. But it also likes to make up its own mind about the rights and wrongs of an issue. Most of us enjoy a riveting or sensational news story and the odd tit-bits of gossip about this personality or that, but we do not always wish to hear the same seedy revelations about the same football manager day in and day out or to be almost constantly reminded of the unsavoury side of life.

The news media underestimates its readers and viewers. It assumes the British public invariably wants to read about tragedy, mishaps and man's inhumanity to man. When Martyn Lewis, the BBC newsreader, suggested in an article that people might be interested in stories about achievements, goodwill and acts of kindness there was a general outcry by the press, who dismissed Lewis's claims as unrealistic and out of touch, but he had made an important point. The news media is reluctant to find out what the public really wants to see, read or hear or to assess its own role as a responsible communicator.

Very rarely does the media sit back and reflect on what is significant and what is not, or even delve for the real truth behind an issue. The result is that the general public is under-educated in its understanding of events, tending to believe everything it reads or hears, some of which is blatantly misleading or untrue. It is only when the puppet-master makes a glaring error or libels a public person that we ever have a hint of his frailty.

Perhaps the most fickle characteristic of today's news media is the many roles its journalists play. Reporters, sub-editors and editors are supposed to be able to write or report on almost any given subject. Like a good barrister, a journalist must have the ability to master a brief – or, in this case, a story – very quickly and then express it clearly and articulately. It is like a game of instant punditry. Sum up European federalism in fifty words; describe the role of the monarchy in two easy phrases; write a caption summing up the pros and cons of Post Office privatization. Even in technical journalism, where journalists are called on to write about everything from water softeners to nuclear reactors, many know only a little about a huge range of specialist subjects. This can lead to exaggeration, distortion and inaccuracy – and gives many journalists a false air of superiority.

The privilege of being able to write and commentate for a large public also tends to give journalists an inflated outlook. Today's columnists and commentators wield a powerful hold over their audiences. But, because they cannot be challenged until their views have appeared, they do not always give those audiences the respect they deserve, some using their columns or television shows as glorified ego-trips to impress journalists on rival newspapers and networks. Yet people continue to regard their views as sacred. Theatre critics such as Clive Barnes and Frank Rich of the *New York Times* can make or break a Broadway production with a few choice words of invective.

The seemingly straightforward reporting of events has been transformed in the 32 years since the Profumo Scandal. Before the 1960s, the average newspaper report was concise and simple with no unnecessary adjectives or showy sentences. It reflected the words of C P Scott, the famous *Guardian* editor, who once told his reporters: 'Comment is free, but facts are sacred.' Newspaper and radio reporters took a pride in getting the facts of a story and presenting it as clearly as possible – whether it was the scene of a fire, a shipwreck, a factory take-over or a parliamentary report. Reading pre-1960s copies of popular newspapers such as the *News Chronicle* or the *Daily Mail*, you are immediately impressed by the sharpness and detail of their reports. Suddenly the news has a *frisson* of urgency and excitement.

Today it is sometimes hard for the reader or viewer to get an accurate picture of an event, let alone a *frisson* of excitement. Instead of striving for objectivity, many stories are coloured by proprietorial interference, political bias, the editor's prejudices and the reporter's colourful imagination, leaving the public with a distorted view of an event. C P Scott would not have approved.

In the past three decades, another factor has emerged – the popular news media's insatiable need to exaggerate and shock to attract new readers, listeners and viewers. Several newspapers and programmes have become powers unto themselves and their readers rather than responsible commentators.

In 1837, the writer Thomas Carlyle described newspapers as the fourth estate, members of the British Establishment, as indispensable as the other three estates: the aristocracy, the House of Commons and the Church. With few exceptions, they maintained this reputation during the nineteenth and early twentieth centuries, and the great newspaper proprietors of the 1920s and 1930s, Lords Beaverbrook, Rothermere, Northcliffe and Kemsley certainly believed their newspapers were the fourth estate, even if for the wrong reasons, when they used them to express their political opinions and enhance their personal standing in public life. Today, newspapers still believe they are Britain's official commentators. Some of them still have a laudable sense of responsibility; but the free-spirited thinking and independence of the early 1900s – later typified by *The Times* in the 1960s and the *Independent* in the late 1980s – has been subdued by commercialism and circulation wars in a fiercely competitive mass market.

There are glimmers of hope. We can still find sections of the media – notably some of the quality newspapers, television and radio – that pride themselves on their defence of democracy and the public's right to know. They use these causes to promote journalistic campaigns and cases of compassion and to highlight the plight of the poor and oppressed. Such media attention not only alerts the authorities, but often prompts new legislation on social issues. However these principles sometimes become convenient clichés for editors and producers when they are trying to justify their actions or to get out of a tight corner over, say, an attack on a government minister or some seedy revelations about a pop star's private life. Phrases such as 'defence of democracy' and the 'public's right to know' sound impressively concerned in media columns and right-of-reply television programmes.

One media cause that has remained consistent throughout history is its role as a government watchdog. This has hardly wavered from the first days of *The Times* and its tiny band of home news reporters in 1785 to today's television leviathan whose satellites and cables have created a new British space and underground network. The news media's aloofness from other British institutions enables it to challenge government policy, condemn poor decisions (and occasionally praise good ones), and generally act as a second opposition in a two-party system. Some would argue that over such issues as European unity and taxation, the news media has proved more effective than Her Majesty's Opposition. There is a danger, however. Even in their watchdog role, newspapers, television and radio sometimes overstep the mark and become superior grand inquisitors. Yet another example of the trappings of power.

The news media can also be a masterful interrogator. It can uncover examples of sleaze such as illegal payments to MPs for questions in parliament, the use of 'bungs' to players and football managers during transfer deals, excessive salaries paid to some heads of public companies, and the rising number of company frauds and computer-hacking cases. With a fanfare of campaigning zeal, the news media can use its resources to expose these corrupt practices and injustices in front-page news items or face-to-face television interviews. It is a vital democratic safeguard. There is an ever-present danger, however, of turning an ordinary issue into a national crisis.

The British news media's independence is its greatest strength. But it does not always appreciate this. It likes to appear as the grand defender of democracy rather than the trusty voice of the people and shows little humility when justifying its actions over serious issues that affect people's lives and livelihoods.

The British are avid readers, listeners and viewers – a trend that will continue with growing leisure time and moments of escape from job and family problems, recessions and balance-of-payments crises. We have a more varied range of national newspapers and magazines than any other Western country, catering for almost every taste, class and educational standard; we also have the world's highest readership, with 60 per cent of the British public reading a newspaper at some stage of the day.

At the start of the 1990s recession, there were fears that sales of national daily and Sunday papers were seriously dwindling, with a total fall of 400,000 a day for the dailies and 900,000 for the Sundays since 1980. This was partly due to an influx of local radio stations and multi-channel cable TV networks able to carry live news flashes and reports on events as they occurred. But the outlook remains bright. The British are creatures of habit, enjoying the luxury of their daily, evening and Sunday newspapers, and the growing nuclei of local newspapers and free-sheets that drop through the letterbox each week. Readership is falling slightly, but British newspapers will continue to entertain and inform the reading public well into the next century, despite greater competition from rival media networks and steadily rising newsprint costs. The advertisers who were numbed by the recession of the early 1990s are now helping to put money back into the news media coffers.

Business entrepreneurs know newspapers make money. Papers are always opening and closing and reappearing in different guises, according to the trends of the market and the hunches of their proprietors. Entrepreneurs also know that, if strategically planned and astutely managed, television channels and radio stations prosper, so they too are always opening, often being taken over and rarely closing, their advertisers recognizing a good market when they see one.

In an age of mass communications, television, radio and newspapers have become more than informers, entertainers and money-makers. They have become trendsetters, with the resources to pry into the most intimate of lives and the most public of institutions – sometimes with dire or embarrassing consequences. Today's media proprietors can use their companies as power bases to help expand their business empires, pledging support for trading policies and government regimes in their newspapers one day so as to aid new acquisitions the next. They can also use their media holdings to boost each other, witness Rupert Murdoch's unashamed newspaper promotions of his television station, BSkyB.

The British news media has another valuable asset: freedom. Since the Second World War, the media has been able to work and act almost unheeded. In the absence of a written constitution and with few government checks and balances, it can say or write almost what it likes – with the added bonus of new technology and a national proclivity for sleaze. The only legal hurdles to complete freedom of speech are the Obscene Publications Act, the Official Secrets Acts and the laws of libel, privilege and contempt. Otherwise, the media has only its conscience, a few vested interests, and the reading habits of the public to answer to.

Governments have been notoriously faint-hearted about curbing the powers of the news media. They fear a backlash from the voters, the establishment and the opposition and do not wish to rid themselves of the political advantages of a free press. In the past 50 years there have been three government commissions into the role of the fourth estate. All were inconclusive. Of the four committees on broadcasting since 1945, only two so much as caused a ripple of excitement – the

1977 Annan Report which recommended the setting up of
Channel Four and the 1986 Peacock Report which led to an
increase in the BBC's licence fee.

Several MPs have recently tried to introduce privacy
legislation. All were unsuccessful. The majority of Conservative
MPs do not wish to curb their main source of propaganda or to
lose favour with the party's large pro-freedom lobby. Even the
Calcutt Committee, set up in 1990 to consider the need for new
privacy laws, merely recommended that the 37-year-old Press
Council should change its name to the Press Complaints
Commission.

However, the new Commission has no legislative role.
Neither does it have the Press Council's authority as a defender
of press freedom. It can only condemn newspapers for what it
considers to be irresponsible behaviour. The news media's
other main self-regulator, the Broadcasting Complaints
Commission, was introduced in 1981, and serves a similar role
in television and radio. Both commissions are staffed by senior
journalists, broadcasters and public figures, their aim being to
give individuals or institutions the chance to gain redress for
what they consider to be ill-treatment or invasion of privacy.
The only other media self-regulators are ombudsmen, who
were appointed by a committee of editors in 1989 to ensure
that the main newspapers keep to a nationally agreed Code of
Practice, correcting their own newspapers' mistakes and
creating a self-conscious brouhaha if they fail to act in the
public interest.

Thus far, calls for a Freedom of Information Act – similar to
the US version of 1966 – have been ignored. If it were
introduced, it would give the news media access to a far greater
number of security-vetted official documents, whether parliamentary, civil service or industrial, and help to keep the general
public better informed about the workings of government and
industry.

It is unlikely that the British government will change its need
for secrecy and bureaucracy. The repeated leaking of
documents from parliament and Whitehall has made the

government increasingly security-sensitive and reticent. Rather than relaxing its attitude, leaks have made it even less likely to reveal information and, on a more personal level, for MPs to declare their business interests unless forced to do so by a persistent media. This has created a growing barrier between government and press and made journalists increasingly irascible, outspoken and intrusive. It is not surprising that stories about state secrets surge forth; that media coverage becomes more speculative and sensational as it weaves its way round this hidden trove of information. The final irony is that, despite recent initiatives to create more open government, many cover-ups are only revealed when the government is forced to set up public investigations such as the 1994 Scott Inquiry into secret arms trading or the 1995 Nolan Inquiry into government sleaze. The news media then realizes it has been duped out of a series of genuine public interest stories. Though the news media later got its own back by printing leaked extracts of the Scott Report before it was officially published.

The news media revolution really began in 1963 when the Profumo Scandal shook the first, second and third estates out of their post-war inertia and made Britain realize that it was as fallible as its European neighbours. After Profumo, the popular newspapers used five main themes to entice their readers – sex, royalty, animals, sport and crime – led by the *News of the World*, the world's largest-selling (and perhaps most prurient) Sunday newspaper. The media's more racy approach to the news was also inspired by a decade of free thought, self-discovery and adventure.

In the 1970s, the media used another theme to titillate its readers: the eccentric activities of homo sapiens. One day it might be a local man who had decided to put up a windmill in his garden, ruffling both the hedges and sensitivities of his neighbours, the next the denigration of a famous poet whose glorious verses were found to have been copied from the writings of a hermit living in obscurity in a tiny Welsh hamlet. Following the lead of the permissive 1960s, the 1970s was the decade when post-war morals began to waver. School, college and university-leavers were more interested in self-expression and independence than traditional values and the family unit. It wasn't cool to live at home after the age of 21 or to join your family at the parish church on Sunday.

The 1980s was the Angry Decade. It saw the growth of a new anarchist youth movement, which attacked the entire British system, dismissing the news media as superficial and the institutions of Church, law, royalty and government as archaic. The essence of being was reduced to spiky locks, raggedy clothes and discordant music. The 1980s was also the Me Decade, in which the popular sentiment, inspired by the American writer Tom Wolfe, was every man for himself. It was regarded as trendy to criticize public figures. Led by the *Sun* and the tabloids, the Angry Eighties spawned a succession of stories about the private lives and loves of politicians, drug-taking pop stars, straying actors and actresses and the indiscretions of the royal family. The traditional media view that politicians were accountable for their policies and little else and that the royal family were respected figureheads had vanished. It was time to debunk, devalue and denigrate.

In the 1990s, the news media has been able to get away with almost anything in the name of the public's right to know. In only a few years it has managed to reverse many of the benefits of a free press, stray precariously from the original aims of the fourth estate and undermine the age-old values of liberty, fraternity and equality. It gives a slightly ironic ring to the nineteenth-century prime minister William Gladstone's view that, 'The freedom of the press is not merely to be permitted and tolerated, but to be highly prized, for it tends to bring closer together all the national interests, and preserves the institutions of the country.'

Today's tabloids are the wolves of the establishment. They have created and perpetuated a climate of sleaze, doing the country a service by revealing misdemeanours in the system and a disservice by constantly ridiculing those who are meant to be running it. At the merest hint of suspicion, the media will slaver and gloat over the lives of footballers and football managers, prime ministers and politicians and the proverbial public personality. Instead of receiving a fair hearing in the news media, many public figures are given a trial by press. Today's tabloids will flaunt the libel laws in the cause of a good story, knowing they have the resources to pay for expensive libel lawyers and high court costs. They are also confident that the readership and circulation gained will outweigh the effects of any bad publicity. Every British tabloid keeps dossiers on top people's private lives which it will publish at the slightest provocation. As Anthony Sampson says in his book *The Essential Anatomy of Britain*: 'Press power was becoming cruder ... as owners and editors collected sexual secrets and waited to reveal them, a tactic which verged on blackmail and effectively intimidated politicians. The players were not interested in checking abuses of power, but in joining in the power-game, and extending their own share.'

Pre-war and post-war values have been replaced by an era of media-ocrity and minimal standards; daily life is faster and more short-term than ever before; slogans stare out at us extolling the merits of washing-up liquids, catalytically converted cars and exotic health foods; and each morning and evening we are roused by the stirring headlines of the news media. A new, more subtle form of media propaganda has emerged in the Nervous Nineties. The Advertorial. This is news blended seamlessly into advertising. By reading about an invasion of dangerous jellyfish in northern Spain, you are lured into booking a two-week holiday on the white, jellyfish-free beaches of southern Spain. The news media has become prey to American marketing techniques. You innocently imagine you are reading an interesting news item when in fact you have become a victim of soft-sell.

The media also plays on our selfish instincts. The tabloid consensus is that it doesn't matter if we corrupt our children or let down our families and fellows provided we can have fun and read stories about the Mata Hari who lures cabinet ministers into five-in-a-bed sessions or the vicar-cum-charity worker who hires out rent-boys to businessmen. Today's tabloids are prepared to push the boundaries of what is acceptable and what is not ever further. Morality and discretion are overlooked in the name of cash-flow and higher readership.

The Fleet Street circulation battle began in 1980 with a vengeance when Rupert Murdoch's *Sun* introduced millionaire bingo. This was quickly followed by Robert Maxwell's version in the *Daily Mirror* which also promised readers a million pounds if they were lucky enough to win. Even *The Times* and *Daily Telegraph* went in for popular, albeit more dignified, games with prizes for the winners – all in the name of higher circulation. Soon television joined the fray with its own viewing wars. Cable television advertised on ITV and Channel Four while, following the example of Murdoch and BSkyB, Associated Newspapers and the Mirror group plugged their own stations, Channel One and WireTV, in their national newspapers.

Murdoch's price war was the most cunning attempt to undermine the opposition. By reducing *The Times* from 45p to 30p in 1993, he succeeded in boosting its circulation by more than 150,000 in less than 12 months. He also forced the qualities' market leader, the *Daily Telegraph*, below its target of one million copies a day, a figure it had exceeded since the start of Max Hastings's editorship in 1985. When *The Times* cut its price to 20p in June 1994, the *Telegraph* responded, reducing its own cover price and restoring nearly all its lost circulation. Murdoch's *Sun*, which was on offer for a penny, then 10p and finally 20p, pushed its circulation well above four million and successfully kept its rival *Daily Mirror* at bay. The *Daily Star* followed suit, but with little success.

The Fleet Street price war was a short-term manoeuvre with a long-term goal – higher circulation. Despite the heavy financial burden on his newspapers (at one stage the *Sun* was losing £1 million a week), Murdoch decided to prolong it, so as to cause maximum damage to his competitors and also to keep his increased market share of the industry.

Modern technology has boosted the news media's selling

power, giving it new, sophisticated methods of presentation and production and hi-tech news-gathering methods. Bugging devices, mobile phones and telephone interception techniques have given reporters new aids to leaked information; telephoto lenses have enabled photographers to pry into people's private lives, whether perched in the boughs of a royal tree, peering over the garden wall into a famous mistress's front room, or tracking a celebrity in an exotic location; and advanced camera equipment has given television viewers a sharper, more penetrating picture of the news, bringing pathos to the fate of famine victims and humour to the antics of young children and pets.

Politicians rely on the media to get their messages across, often opting for skilful presentation rather than serious policy-making to woo the voter round to their way of thinking. Such opportunism has given the news media an unending source of stories and enabled it to reveal some of the more uncaring, hypocritical and Machiavellian methods of British governments and political parties. Every other day a story appears exposing humbug in the corridors of power. Both television and radio cover the House of Commons live, as well as some select committee and House of Lords debates. The quality newspapers and most of the tabloids carry daily news reports, commentaries and parliamentary sketches, while major radio and television programmes such as Radio Four's *Today* and *The World at One* and BBC television's *Panorama* and *Newsnight* grill politicians *ad nauseam*.

A recent media political plaything is the public opinion poll. Most national newspapers run opinion polls – several used to own them as well – and do their best to convince their readers that they accurately reflect the way the country is voting. They are often used for pre-election propaganda by the pro-Tory press, with commentaries by pundits and political correspondents to support them. However, alternative statistical methods show that polls do not always accurately reflect public opinion. The cross-section of people surveyed may not properly represent all three parties; people are also affected by events such as the Falklands War, which swayed a large number of marginal voters from the SDP to the Conservative party. One poll that went badly awry was the MORI Poll just before the 1992 general election which predicted a large Labour victory when in fact the Conservatives won by a sizeable majority.

Polls are one of many sources of news media hype used during general, local and by-elections. Television swingometers, barometers, exit polls and pre-election forecasts veer to and fro as presenters, pundits and panels of experts give their considered opinions; ministers and MPs issue mini-manifestos at showcase rallies; and party candidates are given close scrutiny by sharp-eyed reporters for their dress sense, political beliefs and gaffe-making tendencies.

Newspapers may be able to colour people's political prejudices and dissect the pros and cons of government decisions and policies, but they have little effect on the British public's voting intentions. Most people are pledged to a party through family tradition or political allegiance. The more marginal ones tend to vote through their pockets, with how much tax they are likely to pay or the amount they can expect to earn during a party's term of office being the most important issue. The *Sun*, however, thought otherwise when, after the Conservative victory at the 1992 general election, it grandly announced: 'It's The *Sun* Wot Won It.'

The news media also sees itself as a plausible promoter, reminding its readers about such events as Red Nose Day, Anti-Smoking Week, National Smile Day, National Science Week, and Father's and Mother's Days. It has a talent for rallying causes, giving its readers the opportunity to hear the views of experts on such issues as women's lib (often), men's lib (rarely), gay lib (occasionally), racial equality (often), the environment (often), animal rights (sometimes), Greenpeace (occasionally) and Save the Whale (whenever there is not enough space for Greenpeace). Two political parties, the SDP and the Green Party, would have perished at birth had they not been promoted by an empathetic media. The fashion industry also owes its existence to the media; often the more flamboyant, eccentric and outrageous its creations the better.

In his play *The Title*, Arnold Bennett wrote: 'Journalists say a thing that they know isn't true, in the hope that if they keep on saying it long enough, it *will* be true.' It's a humbling thought. Perhaps we should carry around portable lie detectors and swallow honesty pills to aid our search for authenticity. We are immersed in a confused, hi-tech world of hollow clichés, empty propaganda and shallow jargon. The news media has lost its way. If it is to continue to serve us, we need to redraft its rules.

2

March of the Moguls

'What proprietorship of these papers is aiming at is power, and power without responsibility – the prerogative of the harlot throughout the centuries.'

Stanley Baldwin, paraphrasing Rudyard Kipling

Robert Maxwell thought he was God, Rupert Murdoch believes in God and Conrad Black has some unique theories about our maker. However, the main feature these men share is power. Murdoch, Black and, until 1991, Maxwell own newspaper and television interests that continue to thrive and dominate the global news media. Unlike the newspaper barons of the 1920s and 1930s, Black's and Murdoch's aims are world expansion. Lords Beaverbrook, Northcliffe, Kemsley and the first Lord Rothermere were opinion-makers who liked to try and influence governments with pungent, radical leaders on their front pages. Beaverbrook, or the Beaver as he was known, once shouted to a friend at the Savoy: 'I've got power ... the power of suggestion to millions.' Unlike Beaverbrook, today's

18

tycoons are more interested in empire-building, high circulation and cash-flow than personal or political influence.

Rupert Murdoch is perhaps the most ruthless proprietor in the history of the world news media. Born in Cruden, Victoria, Australia, in 1931, the son of Sir Keith Murdoch, a successful newspaper owner, he went to Geelong grammar school, followed by Oxford University where he gained a third in PPE. His first job was as a sub-editor on the *Daily Express*, popularly known as 'Beaverbrook's brothel'. Then, at the age of 22, the young Rupert took over the running of the *Adelaide News* which he inherited from his father who had died the previous year. It was the start of the most remarkable career in media ownership.

Within three years of joining the *Adelaide News*, Murdoch had carried out his first merger – linking the paper with the larger Adelaide *Sunday Advertiser*. A chubby, bustling figure, he was always hovering over the presses studying typefaces or rolling up his sleeves and goading on his reporters in the newsroom. He was also a party-lover and a gambler. A boy about town. However, the first signs of another side to his character were emerging – his zeal as a cost-cutter. He kept his staff to a minimum and gave all expenses claims his closest scrutiny, a habit which his companies still pursue. He also learnt the value of a good bank, cultivating a long-standing business relationship with the Adelaide branch of the Commonwealth Bank.

At the age of 26, Murdoch married Patricia Booker, an air hostess who lived in Adelaide. After a honeymoon spent looking at several of his properties, the couple settled down, eventually having a daughter, Prudence. But Murdoch was becoming restless. The *News* was doing well. It was time to venture forth. So he went to Melbourne and bought a women's weekly magazine, moving on to Perth where he took over the Perth *Sunday Times* and a series of smaller downtown newspapers. It was the first steps in what William Shawcross describes in his biography, *Rupert Murdoch*, as an 'endless assault on the world'. Murdoch's next goal was television, which had already started to flourish as a popular medium in the United States. He made several reconnaissance trips to the USA to study networks such as ABC and CBS, and opened his own network in Adelaide called Southern Television Corporation.

Then Murdoch lost interest in Adelaide. He wanted more power, more brio, more excitement, to create his own Australian caucus. Murdoch also wanted more cash. He decided to move into the Sydney newspaper market, buying the *Daily* and *Sunday Mirror*s from the huge Fairfax group and turning both papers into sensational tabloids with shock-horror headlines and sexy photographs. The ambitious Murdoch then bought his way into a Sydney television station. 'One tactical or strategic battle followed another, on and on, incessantly moving, questing, searching, striving, fighting, cajoling, bullying, demanding, charming, pushing – always for more. More newspapers, more television, more space, more power,' says Shawcross.

Murdoch's first big creation was *The Australian* which he began in 1964, at the age of 44. It rolled off a second-hand press in Canberra, a serious – or in the words of former *Sun* editor Larry Lamb 'unpopular' – newspaper whose aim was to 'report the nation to Canberra and Canberra to the nation'. This it did effectively, though unprofitably, until Murdoch applied his deft commercial touch, moving the editorial team to Sydney and turning the paper into an Antipodean version of *The Times*. Soon afterwards he fell in love with a junior reporter on the *Sydney Sunday Mirror*, Anna Torv and, after an unhappy divorce from his first wife, the couple were married in 1967.

The following year, Murdoch was invited to London by Sir William Carr, owner of the *News of the World*, who had been anxiously trying to fend off a takeover bid by the owner of Pergamon Press, Robert Maxwell. Murdoch and Carr met at a shareholders' meeting in January 1969. It proved to be more of a showdown than a meeting. Murdoch was given a decisive vote of confidence by the board. He then appointed himself chief executive, increased his shareholding and, six months later, took complete control of the newspaper when, much to Carr's chagrin, Murdoch asked him to stand down as chairman. A typical Murdochian manoeuvre. Murdoch plunged into his new role with gusto, bustling about the office, his sleeves rolled up and shirt slightly ruffled, shedding staff and restrictive practices alike – and, eventually, the editor, Stafford Somerfield.

Soon afterwards another national newspaper fluttered into Murdoch's sights – the *Sun*. Its circulation had fallen from more than one million to 850,000 and its owners, IPC, had offered it to Robert Maxwell for approximately £500,000. The unions had other ideas. They wanted Murdoch. The Australian tycoon outgunned his rival, buying the paper for £800,000. The rest is history. Murdoch's commercial flair shook the *Sun* into profit. Murdoch changed it into a tabloid and created one *Sun* competition after another, the first Page Three Girls, and reader-friendly stories about drug-addicted pop stars, homo-sexual vicars and women of ill repute. The soaraway *Sun* soon became Britain's most successful tabloid under the stewardship of Kelvin Mackenzie, while a bright, scandal-mongering *News of the World* attracted the world's highest Sunday circulation.

A buoyant Murdoch then made his first move into British television, buying shares in and a seat on the board of London Weekend Television. But when he tried to reorganize LWT's programme schedules and become the network's chairman, he was overruled by an Independent Television Authority that was clearly bridled by his cheek.

A pattern was now emerging. The unique feature of Murdoch's deals was his opportunism – the gambler's instinct backed up by a remarkable lucky streak. Murdoch also had a fine reputation with the banks he used, always making his loan repayments on time. Meanwhile his easy charm and impish sense of humour endeared him to all those he dealt with. As Nicholas Coleridge says in his book *Paper Tigers*: 'When he wants to use it, his charm is overwhelming and you can understand how the crocodile of ex-editors, who ever afterwards shake their heads in wonder that they didn't know better, were so easily seduced into working for him.'

Murdoch's global ambitions continued unabated. He wanted to extend his empire into the USA, achieving this in 1973 when he bought three San Antonio newspapers, the *Express*, the *News* and the town's Sunday newspaper. He then launched his own American national, the *Star*, as a direct rival to the sensational *National Enquirer*. However, it was his takeover of *The New York Post*, one of the country's oldest newspapers, that established Murdoch as a leading American entrepreneur.

Back in England, a revolution was stirring. Prompted by high labour costs and the print unions' restrictive practices, media executives were looking at streamlined methods of producing newspapers. However when the Thomson group, owners of *The Times* and *Sunday Times*, threatened to introduce computerization, the typesetters, who were members of the National Graphical Association, took evasive action, staging numerous go-slows and stoppages. Finally the Thomson group lost patience and closed down *The Times* and *Sunday Times* in November 1978. After a lay-off costing £40 million, the two newspapers reopened a year later. But the union stoppages continued and, by autumn 1980, the year's losses totalled nearly £15 million. Drastic action was needed. Thomsons decided to put the newspapers up for sale. Among the interested parties were Lord Rothermere, owner of Associated Newspapers, Lord Matthews of the Express group, Robert Maxwell, owner of Pergamon Press, and Murdoch. A consortium from the two newspapers also put in their own bid.

After several meetings between Thomson executives and the potential bidders, there followed perhaps the most hectic two days in newspaper-ownership history. Murdoch, the favourite because of his previous record, upped his initial offer of £1 million to £12 million and gave several guarantees of editorial independence. The committee appointed to vet the sale was impressed, but Murdoch was unhappy with Thomson's figures and gave the directors a fifteen-minute deadline to produce an accurate balance sheet or, he said, he would call off the deal. As one observer put it: 'The walls dripped with blood'. After a long and hot-tempered meeting, the contract was signed soon after midnight on 21 January 1981.

The union troubles went on, however. Britain was facing the worst recession since the war and the papers were losing money. So Murdoch sacked many of the advertising staff and soon afterwards the newspapers' editors, Harold Evans of *The Times* and Frank Giles of the *Sunday Times*. But there were still problems and Murdoch wanted more than 600 redundancies on the print side to help make the two papers profitable. He needed to find a new solution.

By now other schemes were occupying the tycoon's mind. After buying the profitable *Boston Herald* and several more US newspapers, Murdoch returned to London and bought shares in Sky Television. It was to prove a very shrewd move – the television station, which at the time was a considerable loss-maker, became one of his most valuable assets. No sooner had Murdoch closed the deal, than he returned to America and carried out two of his biggest media coups, buying half of Twentieth-Century Fox, the Hollywood-based film and television group, and Metromedia, a chain of independent television stations.

It was then that one of the most important events in British newspaper history occurred. Murdoch needed money to support his takeovers of Twentieth-Century Fox and Metro-media. Though *The Times*'s circulation was rising and his other three newspapers, the *Sun*, the *News of the World* and the *Sunday Times*, were making money, he saw they had the potential to be very profitable indeed. The answer was to streamline the printing operation – by directly inputting all words and photographs into a computer system – thus avoiding the need for typesetters.

Murdoch and his advisers knew it was a dangerous – if necessary – move. He asked his chief executive, Bert Hardy, to search for a new printing site in London. After several weeks, Hardy discovered a neglected conservation area in Wapping, east London, near the Tower of London. After gaining planning permission to build on the site, Murdoch gave the go-ahead for a new printing plant. It was built within a few months. Then he and his directors held secret talks with the electricians' union and persuaded them to allow their members to develop a radical new computer system.

Fearing a loss of approximately 6,000 jobs, the print unions fought defiantly against the plan. So Murdoch went undercover. Barbed wire was coiled round the fences surrounding the Wapping site and guards were placed at strategic points. A series of fiery meetings was held by the chapels of the National Union of Journalists. Finally, the journalists on the four papers agreed by a majority vote to work at the new site, the first 50 moving to their desks at Wapping in January 1986. Gradually the others joined their colleagues. The new computer system was in place and the presses were ready to roll.

Then the trouble began. Night after night members of the NGA and SOGAT, the two print unions, picketed the Wapping site, hurling rocks, bottles and smoke bombs at police and guards and trying to stop distribution lorries leaving the premises. During the rioting, several pickets and passers-by were injured. Soon a number of disillusioned journalists had left for rival newspapers. Murdoch offered the sacked printers a £50 million redundancy package, but they turned it down. Then in January 1987, almost a year after the troubles began, he upped the offer to £60 million. The printers accepted and the dispute came to a close.

The siege of Wapping was part of the British print revolution. Murdoch had proved that, aided by weak trade union laws, he could take on the powerful unions and win. One after another Fleet Street's newspapers adopted the new technology. As a result, thousands of printers were made redundant during several years of bitterness in the industry.

Murdoch's next British acquisition was *Today* newspaper. Tiny Rowland, then chief executive of Lonrho, had bought it from its founder, Eddie Shah, in 1986, and wanted to sell it on. In 1987, Rowland contacted Murdoch and the two tycoons agreed terms for a £40 million deal. Then an article criticizing Lonrho appeared in the *Sunday Times* and Rowland changed his mind. Enter Robert Maxwell. The Czech tycoon offered a down-payment of £10 million plus the repayment of £30 million debts for a 90-per-cent stake in the paper, at the same time persuading Eddie Shah to sell his 10-per-cent interest. It looked as if the deal was his. But Maxwell foolishly telephoned Murdoch and told him of his intentions. Murdoch immediately contacted Rowland and offered better terms. He also discovered that Maxwell was due to make the purchase at 10 am the following Monday. Murdoch quickly arranged for his negotiating team to be at Rowland's office at 7.15 am on the same Monday morning. The team arrived at 7.14. By 10 am the deal had been signed. Maxwell had lost out to Murdoch again and had failed in his bid to own a British national newspaper. The Australian tycoon now owned five Fleet Street papers.

Murdoch's empire grew apace. His predictions about the success of cable television in Britain, a nation of armchair viewers, proved correct. In 1990, the two loss-making television stations, Sky Television and BSB merged to form BSkyB. Within three years the new station was in profit. It now makes more than £100 million a year.

Murdoch continues to run his empire by telephone, fax and fingertip control from all parts of the globe, starting his day at 6.30 in the morning and carrying on until late in the evening, and always prepared to handle each acquisition and crisis head on.

Where will it all end? Rupert Murdoch is now aged 64 and shows no signs of flagging. He says he wants to keep his media empire in the family and, in 1994, his British heir-apparent, Andrew Knight, former chairman of News International plc, was quietly removed as the day-to-day controller of the British operation. Murdoch continues to be elusive and makes rare public appearances. However, his name will live on in the British news media for many years, even if it is only for the fact that he was the man who helped break the power of the print unions.

Robert Maxwell's main problem was that he believed he could out-manoeuvre Rupert Murdoch. A massive man with a huge personality and a mysterious past, his style could not have been more different. Though he had a certain charm, Maxwell preferred to bully people into doing what he wanted. He treated all negotiations – whether adding new companies to his Pergamon Press network or bidding for national newspapers – like a personal vendetta, getting a malicious pleasure from pushing his rivals and his customers to their limits during negotiations and leaving his decisions until the last moment – or until their nerve went.

Maxwell's weakness was his pride. He saw himself as a colossus bestriding the world media stage. It was Maxwell's boastfulness and power hunger that led to his downfall. He became bigger than the businesses he controlled and his deal-making bravado got the better of him. As his debts mounted, he became dishonest and secretive to try to reverse the situation. Eventually the pressure of his debts drove Maxwell into a kind of madness.

Robert Maxwell was born Jan Ludvik Hoch into a Jewish family in 1923 in the small, backward village of Solotvino in Czechoslovakia. His father, Mechel Hoch, was a cattle dealer; his mother Hannah, a bossy, hard-working matriarch, overweeningly ambitious for her two sons and five daughters. The Hoch family lived in a rented two-room house. In the summer they walked barefoot; in winter they shared each other's shoes. Happiness was a different plate of food on Saturdays.

By the age of eight, Maxwell, who went to a local school, could speak fluent Hebrew and was regarded as an intelligent and energetic pupil by his teachers. At that time his village was in the middle of a bitter struggle to survive, its main occupation being meat smuggling, which probably intrigued the young Maxwell. His main teacher was his grandfather who acted as a middleman in the smuggling operation and no doubt gave Maxwell a tip or two.

During the Hitler regime, the village became a haven for Jews, until war broke out in 1939 and Czechoslovakia was invaded by Germany. Seeing no future for their 16-year-old son in Czechoslovakia, Maxwell's parents sent him and his brother, Alex Pearl, to Budapest in Hungary. However, Maxwell secretly left the country, travelling by train to Yugoslavia and Palestine, before sailing to France and joining the Czech Legion, finally landing in Liverpool in May 1940. At first he tried to get a job as a mechanic but was turned down due to lack of technical expertise. Maxwell then joined the British Army where he rose through the ranks and was a 'popular and outstanding' officer, according to his contemporaries. He spent much of the war in France and, during one attack on the Germans, was awarded the Military Cross for bravery. He also met a pretty French interpreter called Elisabeth (Betty) Maynard, who later became his wife.

After the war, Maxwell started his own company, the European Periodicals, Publicity and Advertising Corporation, importing German newspapers and selling them to German prisoners-of-war in Britain. His next venture, the worldwide distribution of scientific journals, marked the start of his entrepreneurial career. 'He was the sun and we were either planets or had to leave,' says one of his employees. In 1954, Maxwell took over a small publishing company called Pergamon Press. By the end of 1957, it was producing 100 scientific journals and books a year. To increase Pergamon's output, Maxwell split its operations between London and the United States and started a family trust in Liechtenstein.

Maxwell's next two ambitions were to become an MP and to own a national newspaper. Rebuffed as a candidate by the Conservative party, he joined Labour and made an instant impression with his curious blend of philanthropy and public relations. Then in 1964 Maxwell discovered the socialist *Daily Herald* was suffering huge losses, so he devised a survival plan, which partly depended on the support of the unions. Fearing Maxwell's takeover would lead to a loss of jobs, the TUC failed to back him and dashed his hopes of newspaper ownership. The same year he stood in the general election as Labour candidate for North Buckinghamshire and won.

In 1968, Maxwell came up against Rupert Murdoch for the

first time when the two tycoons bid for the *News of the World*. The rest is history, Murdoch being preferred because of his outstanding publishing record. Soon afterwards, Maxwell made a bid for the *Sun* newspaper. Again he was out-manoeuvred by the Australian tycoon. Maxwell's mood was further soured when he lost his North Buckinghamshire seat to the Conservatives in the 1970 general election. His brashness, flamboyance and lack of subtlety seriously affected Maxwell's performance in parliamentary debates and constituency surgeries. After the election, he was no longer regarded as a promising politician but as a millionaire who happened to have socialist views.

Further humiliation was heaped on Maxwell when his company, Pergamon, faced three Board of Trade inquiries into alleged discrepancies. When several adverse profiles about his trading methods appeared in the *Sunday Times* he issued a number of writs against the paper. One of the inquiries later described Maxwell in the famous phrase as 'not a person who can be relied on to exercise proper stewardship of a publicly quoted company'.

But the bouncing Czech, as he came to be known, had a habit of silencing his critics. In 1980, at the age of 57, Maxwell bought shares in the British Printing Corporation, Europe's biggest printer, becoming chairman and proprietor the following year. In an exercise reminiscent of Murdoch, he completely revamped the company, cutting both costs and employees at will and turning its huge losses into considerable profits. The takeover also marked a change in Maxwell's business approach – he feuded with the people he espoused to support, the unions. Another Murdochian policy.

The BPC's dispute with its card-carrying typesetters and machine-minders was bitter and disruptive, leading to strikes and lay-offs. Maxwell won a conclusive victory when, in November 1983, he ordered a group of men with sledgehammers to go into the *Radio Times*'s print works and smash it to pieces. Afterwards Maxwell built modern presses and got the magazine rolling again, changing his company's name to the British Printing and Communications Corporation.

He had now acquired a reputation as a ruthless and opportunistic gambler who thought he could out-manoeuvre any rival. He could turn on the charm or bombast at will, according to the needs of the situation, a man 'with so many balls in the air who played God on five telephones', according to one observer. Maxwell wanted to become a hands-on news media tycoon like his rival Rupert Murdoch but, unlike the stewardship of a big business, running a newspaper needs a special kind of talent – an understanding of newspaper production. Murdoch has it. Maxwell did not.

In 1984, sapped by its struggle with the unions, the Mirror group went up for sale. At the time, its six titles, the *Daily Mirror, Sunday Mirror, People, Daily Record, Sunday Record* and *Sporting Life* were together selling a total of 31 million copies a week. At first, Alex Jarratt, chairman of Reed Holdings, the Mirror's parent company, put out feelers for a potential buyer. But no one, not even Maxwell, was prepared to pay the £100 million asking price. So Jarratt floated it on the Stock Exchange, appointing Clive Thornton, former chairman of Abbey National Building Society, as its chairman. However the new company failed to deliver. With almost predictable suddenness, the directors received a phone call from Robert Maxwell.

Maxwell had already tried and failed to win control of *The Times* and *Sunday Times*, mainly due to his doubtful reputation with the establishment, and his 1984 bid for the *Observer* was also foiled by circumstances. This time he was quite resolute. His first offer of £80 million was turned down flat, so he put in another of £100 million. Failing to get a satisfactory answer from Reed's directors, Maxwell bombarded them with phone calls, which did not help their peace of mind or the alcohol level of the nervous *Mirror* journalists. After political interventions from Labour MPs Michael Foot and Roy Hattersley, who wanted the *Daily Mirror* to remain a party supporter, the Reed board decided to sell the papers to the former Labour MP for £90 million.

His Mirror group acquisition led to Maxwell's biggest

self-promotion campaign. Its theme was The Colossus Rides Again. In a parody of the late Lord Beaverbrook, Maxwell's picture appeared almost daily on the *Daily Mirror*'s front page. One day he would be greeting a president, the next starring in a glittering national celebration, the Czech tycoon bemusing a bewildered Britain with his views on the government's foreign policy, trade, sport, health, environment, Britain's future and, of course, Maxwell himself. The *Daily Mirror*'s rivals called the paper the *Daily Maxwell*. Despite the razzmatazz, the paper's circulation fell from 3.4 million to 2.9 million. Though Maxwell succeeded in being the first news media owner to feature high-quality colour in a national newspaper, he failed in his bid to overtake, let alone approach, the circulation of Murdoch's *Sun*.

Yet Maxwell still believed he could outshine Murdoch with his own £5 billion global communications network. His first step was to rename BPCC, MCC (Maxwell Communications Corporation), after the famous British cricket club with the same initials. His second was to start a 24-hour newspaper, the *London Daily News*. But it folded five months later, after a clever spoiling operation by Lord Rothermere who launched a cheaper and newsier rival. Despite this setback, Maxwell's news media holdings in 1987 were considerable. He owned the Mirror group, 20 per cent of Central Television, 15 per cent of Border Television, 12½ per cent of a French television channel, and a British cable station. Yet beneath the prosperous veneer, his debts were rising. Despite daily competitions, price-cutting and pledges of aid to under-developed countries, the *Daily Mirror*'s circulation stayed more than half a million below the *Sun*'s.

Maxwell's last three big ventures were probably his most audacious. *The European* newspaper, which he started in a blaze of publicity in 1989, was losing £2 million a month by the following year; the joint purchase of Macmillan the publishers and the *Official Airline Guide* in the USA cost him £2 billion and only increased his borrowings with little immediate return; while his pledge to turn round the loss-making *New York Daily*

News was yet another drain on his health and finances. Maxwell's deal-making was finally getting the better of him and several months later he died in mysterious circumstances.

The Canadian, Conrad Black, is one of the new breed of British media tycoons. He owns 240 newspapers, compared with Rupert Murdoch's 125. However, they are mainly Canadian and North American small circulation papers, unlike Murdoch's more upmarket versions. Black is tall, well-built and distinguished-looking and invariably cheerful. He is also the most intellectual of the tycoons. He has three Canadian degrees – in history from Carleton and McGill universities and in law from Laval – and is the author of a 743-page biography of Maurice Deplessis, the former Quebec premier. An irrepressible acquisitor, Black regards newspapers as a licence to make history and heads the fastest-growing newspaper empire in the world.

In 1985, he received a phone call in his Canadian office from Andrew Knight, editor of *The Economist*, who was looking for a suitor for the ailing Telegraph group. Black showed interest and sent his lawyer, Daniel Colson, to England to discuss a possible deal with Lord Hartwell and the Berry family, the group's owners since 1927. they offered Black a £10 million shareholding. However the Telegraph group, which included the *Daily* and *Sunday Telegraph*s and the *Spectator*, needed more financial support. After several months of negotiations, during which Black came to London only twice, the owners offered him a £30 million holding which gave him 50.1 per cent control of the group. He accepted.

One observer said the takeover needed a 'very substantial quotient of luck and also good nerve on Black's part, because it wasn't clear then that it would work out so well'. But despite his bravura, Black found the group was verging on bankruptcy. The two *Telegraph*s, which were then based at 135 Fleet Street, were traditional, dull and unenterprising and the group's respectable façade hid laid-back marketing methods, overmanning and a wastage of resources.

Black moved the *Telegraph*s to open-plan offices in South

Quay, a multi-storey block in the Isle of Dogs, and later to nearby Canary Wharf. He made Andrew Knight his chief executive and appointed two strong-minded right-wingers, Max Hastings and Peregrine Worsthorne, editors of the *Daily* and *Sunday* respectively. He finished modernizing the printing plant and, following Murdoch's union-bashing efforts at Wapping, introduced new technology, laying off a large number of journalists, advertising and circulation staff. He turned the *Telegraph*s into attractively written broadsheets and, helped by the editorial and marketing flair of editor Max Hastings, kept the *Daily Telegraph*'s circulation above the one million mark – almost the combined circulation of *The Times, Guardian* and *Independent* – introducing personality stories to attract a younger readership.

In 1989, Black bought the *Jerusalem Post*, negotiating the deal from London. At one stage, Maxwell entered the fray, but his bid was turned down, the Czech tycoon later phoning Black to say he had graciously decided not to top his offer. Another example of Maxwellian bombast. During the 1980s, Black added the Fairfax group's *Sydney Morning Herald, Melbourne Age* and *Australian Financial Review* to his growing empire.

Between 1985 and 1992, he spent £119 million building up an 83-per-cent stake in the Telegraph group, finally floating it on the Stock Exchange which gave Hollinger, his holding company, 68 per cent of the newspapers' shares. In the early 1990s, the group's pre-tax profits averaged around £40 million a year, and it was valued at around half a billion pounds. Though profits temporarily dived during the circulation wars, they soon recovered their former strength.

No story of today's tycoons would be complete without a mention of its two barons, Lords Rothermere and Stevens. Lord Rothermere, son of the first Lord Rothermere, is the newspaper industry's equivalent of a gentleman-tycoon. When he was offered the chance of buying the *Observer* he turned it down because it didn't feel right. That little episode sums up the man – rich, instinctive and easy-going, not the lean and power-hungry mogul ready to pounce on any opportunity that arises. Rothermere owns newspapers for the pleasure of it. He likes the company of journalists and enjoys the strategies of the industry. When he took over the *Daily Mail* from his father in 1978, he gave the journalists the best offices and the biggest expense accounts in the company – believing that as creative individuals they deserved special treatment.

Rothermere owns three successful British newspapers, the *Daily Mail*, the *Mail on Sunday* and the London *Evening Standard*, and relies on his chairman, Sir David English, a former *Daily Express* foreign editor, to do much of the day-to-day running. Their relationship is based on mutual respect. Rothermere provides much of the overall strategy and English the editorial drive.

Though Rothermere spends most of the year in Paris and Kyoto, Japan, only appearing in Britain for about 90 days for tax reasons, he uses his days in residence to carry out his keenest strategies. The first was in 1972 when he decided to change the *Daily Mail* from broadsheet to tabloid, a dramatic move that made its chief rival the *Daily Express*, a broadsheet with double the *Mail*'s circulation, look old-fashioned. Rothermere saw that the middle-market commuter and home-maker was ready for a compact newspaper. Before long, the *Daily Mail* was drastically reducing the *Express*'s lead.

Rothermere's second ingenious strategy was his purchase of the loss-making London *Evening Standard* from the Trafalgar House group. In 1977, Rothermere had been offered the newspaper by its then owners, Beaverbrook Newspapers, and agreed a figure of £7.5 million. However when news of the deal leaked out, Fleet Street was overcome by anti-merger madness. Amid the uncertainty the Beaverbrook group was scooped up by the shipping firm Trafalgar House, and the *Evening Standard* remained intact for the next three years. Then, in 1980, Rothermere was approached again. He agreed to close his own London evening newspaper, the *Evening News*, in return for a 50 per cent stake in the *Standard*. He later bought it outright and transformed it into a commercial and journalistic success.

Lord Stevens of Ludgate is perhaps the least likely tycoon of Fleet Street. Most of his life has been spent as a fund manager, and he became a newspaper proprietor by chance when he was appointed chairman of United Newspapers in 1981. Under his direction the company has grown apace. Apart from owning the *Daily Express*, *Sunday Express* and the *Daily Star*, United has 121 British regional newspapers and 11 in eastern Spain. Its total circulation is even higher than Conrad Black's newspaper empire.

The main difference between Stevens and the other big proprietors is that he does not have a majority holding in the company he chairs, United Newspapers. However he is perhaps the most budget-led proprietor. Soon after becoming chairman of United Newspapers, he realized their profits covered too limited an area, so he started a nationwide chain of free newspapers, acquired *Exchange and Mart*, and expanded into the USA, buying Newswire, a satellite-based communications network, and two publications in New York and San Francisco. Anyone who spends a day with Lord Stevens will discover he is more interested in ensuring his newspapers keep within their budgets, without high expense accounts and glamorous overseas trips, than making great play about the thrills of empire-building.

Stevens likes to be seen to be running his national newspapers, spending much of his time at United Newspapers' headquarters on London's Blackfriars Bridge, only a few hundred yards from Fleet Street, as opposed to his financial head office in the city. He holds fortnightly lunches for his editors when he suggests ideas for stories that he meticulously follows through from galley-proof stage to final publication. He also likes to put his reporters and columnists right on current affairs and subjects he knows about. Whenever a story attracts or offends him, he sends a note to the journalist who wrote it. Though a keen low-handicap golfer, Stevens has only had three complete days off work to play golf in the past 34 years.

To some media people, Stevens is the unknown proprietor. But such a reputation can have its merits. Once at an important dinner party, the wife of a prominent politician berated Stevens about the news-gathering tactics of the *Evening Standard*. This went on for several minutes until, during a lull in the conversation, Stevens quietly pointed out that he did not in fact own the *Evening Standard*. She had got the wrong proprietor.

The journalist Hannen Swaffer said in 1928: 'Freedom of the press in Britain is freedom to print such of the proprietor's prejudices as the advertisers don't object to.' Until the mid-1970s, he was correct. But today's owners are more interested in possession than mere prejudice, using their newspapers and television networks to further their commercial interests and sometimes showing scant regard for recognized business practices in their pursuit of power. In Britain the expanding news media is falling into the hands of fewer and fewer tycoons. At present there are laws restricting cross-media ownership, though, with his American passport, Rupert Murdoch manages to bypass a number of these. The true power of the modern media owner was shown when, in 1994, the tycoon Silvio Berlusconi became Italy's prime minister by promoting himself through his own news networks. Britain is not far behind. If the UK weakens its cross-media laws, a future leader at Number 10 may own the very news media that put him there.

3

Who Calls the Shots?

'Newspaper editors are men who separate the wheat from the chaff, and then print the chaff.'

Adlai Stevenson

Newspaper editors, shepherds and lighthouse-keepers have one thing in common – they all hold down lonely jobs. The solitary roles of the last two are created by nature and the elements, while the first faces a lone daily battle with deadlines, commerce, his proprietor and public opinion. If anything goes wrong, he or she has to suffer the consequences, as many great editors of the past have found to their cost. The reward, however, is the final flowering of a successful career in journalism.

Editors are men – or women – of many parts. They control the way newspapers gather and present the news and have the final say over their daily content, often using leader columns to project their views on such topical issues as the royal family, government policies, the price of iceberg lettuces and the merits of traffic cones. The only person who can overrule an editor's decisions is the newspaper proprietor.

There are two types of Fleet Street editor. The first sees himself or herself as a thinking person's guide to world events. He regards journalism as a serious business with a message to pass on to the reader. The second looks on his job as a branch of show-business, behaving more like an actor-manager than an earnest commentator and judging stories more for their entertainment value than their intrinsic newsworthiness. Whereas the serious editor attempts to find out what a public figure is trying to say, the popular one wants to know what he or she is trying to hide.

The newspaper's editorial direction is usually a subtle blend of the proprietor's wishes and vested interests and the editor's instincts. Together, they may wish to support the government over privatization, attack the power and fuel industries, back a regime in South America or run an exposé on an actress's private life. It depends on the pressure of circumstance, changing trends in readership and a connection or two in high places. During general elections some of the most independent of newspapers can become thinly disguised versions of party manifestos.

Many of today's editors preside over clinical, open-plan offices where reporters and sub-editors sit intently in front of rows of featureless computer terminals. The prose is generally white instead of purple and the humour grey as opposed to black. Working in newspapers has become an intense commercial business, indulged in by solemn, pale-faced men and women, an occupation where the trivial pursuit of dinosaurs, doctrines and *la dolce vita* has become relatively humourless.

In common with many large organizations, walking into the offices of a national newspaper is a little like entering a medium-security jail. Every staff member has to pass through a tight security cordon at the reception desk where, after satisfying a uniformed official he is not carrying anything illegal or dangerous, he must produce an identity card bearing his photograph. If he has forgotten it, security must telephone the newspaper's personnel department to confirm his identity. Visitors face even stricter scrutiny. They too are searched, sometimes more rigorously. Then they must give the nature of their business and the name of the person with whom they have an appointment. Security then phone the appointee to confirm that a meeting has been arranged. If the visitor cannot satisfy the newspaper's entry requirements he is turned away.

The tight cordon is to protect newspapers against a rising number of bomb scares and security leaks in the past decade. By the time the visitor has risen seven floors in the lift, passed through the goggle-eyed curiosity of a wall-less, fluorescent void and been scrutinized by more uniformed officials and journalists, he feels about two feet tall. He could be forgiven for thinking Big Brother is watching through a fish-eye lens.

Gone are the days of turning up for work in shabby local newspaper offices where the paper is peeling off the walls and last night's cigarette butts and empty coffee cups are strewn around the floor. A few bleary-eyed reporters are still yawning and reminiscing about the previous night in the pub, when suddenly at ten o'clock footsteps descend the creaking staircase and the editor arrives and asks for any news items for the ensuing day. Quarter of an hour of laughter and badinage follows while the editor and the chief reporter go through the diary and hand out the day's work. Soon the office becomes a scene of erratic industry, the clattering of typewriters interspersed with animated discussions about Manchester United and cheap jibes about someone's new hairstyle.

Gone is the rumble of the hot-metal and plate-making machines in the printing works below; the pungent smell of printers' ink as the proofs are rushed through; and the roar of the first edition rolling off the presses. Gone, too, is the camaraderie of Fleet Street pubs where reporters and their cronies would spend timeless lunch breaks telling tales of hoaxes, missed deadlines and the general futility of too much hard work.

Journalism has lost much of its sense of fun. Most editors are hidden by the protective shell of their offices where they can linger over the day's pages and maybe reflect on their personal impact on British life. In the open-plan offices outside banter is limited as, amid the tick-tacking of plastic keyboards, reporters and sub-editors try to meet their deadlines in a haze of air-conditioned automation.

A modern editor is a marketing man, as well as a journalist. He has to steer a delicate path between editorial and advertising interests and, occasionally, the will of his proprietor. Today's newspapers are serious, money-making concerns where the editor has less personal influence than he did in the 1950s and 1960s. Like a football manager and his team, he knows his job rests or falls on the success or failure of his product. He must be canny and streetwise, a man able to cater for current consumer trends as well as his readers' fickle tastes. Colour spreads and gripping stories must be supported by promotions, readers' offers, competitions and advertorials.

Another more recent facet of the editor's job is a talent for titillation. As Raymond Snoddy puts it in his book *The Good, the Bad and the Unacceptable*: 'Competition and the pressure to find stories sensational enough to make papers walk off the newsagents' counters encourage invention, exaggeration and the invasion of privacy.' Some newspaper editors spend hundreds of thousands, even millions, of pounds a year on cheque-book journalism or stories that can be bought for a negotiable fee, as well as stories that never appear or fail to come off. Fiction is an editorial stock-in-trade, though not all stories are as far-fetched as a recent *Sunday Sport* report about the inhabitants of a Cornish village being forced to flee after an invasion of man-eating spiders that ate the postmaster's daughter and her fiancé while they were sunbathing in the back garden.

An editor's efforts to entertain can end in tears – as a *Daily Star* editor found when he went to the aid of a lovesick polar bear. Lucky the bear had been pining at Chester Zoo after the death of his mate. So, in the interests of a good story, the editor decided to send a team of bear-catchers to the North Pole to find him a new mate. They duly found and captured a likely-looking female and brought her back to England. As the romantic meeting was to take place the following day, the bear's minders decided to hire an icy pool for the night. Like most polar bears, she decided to spend the night on the pool bottom. The following morning, needing air, the polar bear rose to the pool's surface and tried to break through the ice at the top, but hard as she tried she could not do so, and after several attempts, the hapless animal stopped breathing and drowned. When her minders arrived to take her to her love tryst, they saw a notice above the pool pointing out that the thin layer of ice on the surface was in fact a piece of fibreglass. Sadly, it was too late to resuscitate the animal. The *Daily Star*'s editor had wasted valuable manpower and money on a heart-lifting story that never took place.

So what are Britain's national newspaper editors really like? To find the answer we must look at the six dominant personalities of recent years. Kelvin MacKenzie, who ran the *Sun* for 13 years, is a burly, bustling south Londoner; former *Daily Telegraph* editor Max Hastings, the son of two equally famous journalists, Macdonald Hastings and Anne Scott-James, is a lofty, well-spoken former war correspondent; Andrew Neil, *Sunday Times* editor for 11 years, is a bright, pugnacious Scotsman who is now pursuing a successful career as a columnist and television commentator; Andreas Whittam Smith, founder of the *Independent* and *Independent on Sunday*, is a tall, rangy and avuncular former city editor; Sir David English, editor of the *Daily Mail* from 1972 to 1992, is a dapper and dynamic Londoner; while David Montgomery, former *Today* and *News of the World* editor, is a slim, fast-talking Irishman.

As editor of the *Sun* between 1981 and 1994, Kelvin Calder MacKenzie dared to probe further than any other tabloid editor had probed before. MacKenzie's audacious editorship created a newspaper style that was both revolutionary and mind-boggling. The son of two south London journalists, he originally worked on a local paper and at a Kent news agency before joining the *Daily Express* as a sub-editor. Known to his colleagues as Macca, Mackenzie's rasping south London tones and typographical skills amused and amazed his superiors. He moved to the *Sun* where Rupert Murdoch picked him out as a man with prospects, sending him to the USA as managing editor of *The New York Post*. However Macca's wife and family soon hankered after the English way of life, so he asked for a transfer and was appointed deputy night editor of the *Sun*. Soon his eye for a story became the talk of the office and he was wooed away by the *Daily Express* who made him their night news editor. However the *Sun* would not release Macca from his contract, so he found he was working on both newspapers, finishing his shift on one to cross the Fleet Street traffic later in the day to take up his post at the other. During this period, more discerning readers of the two newspapers may have noticed similarities in some of their stories. Finally, in 1981 Murdoch talked Macca, then aged 34, into becoming editor of the *Sun*.

The next 13 years were like a one-man crusade as Macca and his men carried out a high-powered campaign of shock, horror and titillation. The *Sun*'s racy journalism overshadowed the other Fleet Street tabloids. In one desperate leader, the *Daily Mirror* described its rival as 'the harlot of Fleet Street'. Many of the *Sun*'s critics believed it was living off immoral earnings.

Macca's favourite name for the *Sun* was the cockney phrase 'The Currant Bun'. The paper became the talk of pubs, clubs and sleaze-happy families throughout Britain. By December 1988, the paper's circulation had reached 4.3 million, only fractionally under its 1994 peak of 4.4 million. If ever he was asked to describe a typical *Sun* reader, Macca would use the language of advertising and call him a C2, comparing him to the AB1s who read *The Times, Guardian* and *Independent*. When Fleet Street's newspaper editors set up a code of practice to try to curb the rising tide of scandal, Macca dismissed it as a 'load of bollocks'.

Max Hastings went to Charterhouse before winning an exhibition to Oxford. He worked for the BBC and became foreign correspondent of the London *Evening Standard*, bivouacking his way to the Front ahead of his rivals during the

Falklands War. He was appointed editor of the *Daily Telegraph* in 1985, replacing William (now Lord) Deedes, a former Conservative minister who still writes for the *Telegraph*. During Deedes's editorship, the *Telegraph* earned the sobriquet, the 'Torygraph'. Hastings himself is a radical right-winger, unafraid to support sanctions against President Botha's regime in South Africa and to criticize the Tory government on occasions.

When Hastings took over, the *Telegraph* became one of the best-written and newsiest papers in Britain. It also has the finest foreign news coverage of the nationals (in the Sixties and Seventies it had the second highest number of foreign correspondents of any newspaper in the world). Hastings and the *Daily Telegraph* chairman Andrew Knight oversaw its move to new premises on the Isle of Dogs as well as the modernization of its nearby printing works. After moving into open-plan premises the *Telegraph* shrugged off its old-boys' club image and became a slick, if slightly yuppie, newspaper. Its previously fusty contents were refined into finely written feature articles, sharp news reporting, in-depth interviews and obituaries that gave a genuine insight into history. Hastings and Knight also added a Weekend supplement in the Saturday *Telegraph* that included almost every aspect of middle- and upper-class life, including stories about stately homes and hunting, shooting and fishing columns; bridge, chess and gardening articles; and the latest fads in food and wines.

Though *Private Eye* likes to refer to him as Max 'Hitler' Hastings, there is little evidence of the dictator in Hastings, although he is a strong and forthright editor. Now editor of the London *Evening Standard*, Hastings, like his former proprietor, Conrad Black, has a keen interest in military memorabilia and has also written five books on military history. In 1990, he was made editor-in-chief of both the *Daily* and *Sunday Telegraph*s and a member of the *Telegraph* board. He steered the *Daily* astutely through the circulation wars and when, in 1994, it dipped below the one-million mark for the first time in his editorship, he managed to manoeuvre it back over the magic figure again, more than 300,000 ahead of its nearest rival, *The Times*.

Born in Paisley in 1949, Andrew Neil gained an honours degree in politics and economics at Glasgow University. After a short spell as a researcher at Conservative Central Office, he became a government political adviser before joining *The Economist* as lobby correspondent, labour editor, American correspondent and finally editor. During this period, he broadcast regularly on radio and television.

Neil became editor of the *Sunday Times* in 1983 after he went to interview Rupert Murdoch and found they both approved of the deregulation of television. Shortly afterwards, Neil moved with the paper to 'Fortress' Wapping. During the ensuing printing dispute, Neil described the journalists who left the paper as 'the great tribe of the dispossessed'. Under his editorship, the *Sunday Times*'s circulation rose steadily as he turned it into a multi-section newspaper similar to the American Sundays. At the same time the paper sacrificed some of the investigative flair it had shown under Neil's predecessor, Harold Evans. Neil's trademark at the paper's weekly conferences was his infectious enthusiasm and superb news sense. He was also a fanatically hard worker – a hands-on editor in the true sense of the phrase.

In 1988, Neil was appointed executive chairman of Sky Television, editing the *Sunday Times* at the same time as overseeing the launch of four new satellite channels. In 1994, Neil left the paper for a seven-month stint on Murdoch's Fox Television station in the USA. The venture did not work out, however. After a combined £1 million pay-off from the two jobs, Neil returned to England to work as a freelance and develop his other media talents.

Andreas Whittam Smith was born in 1937, the son of a canon, and educated at Birkenhead School and Keble College, Oxford. At the age of 25 he joined the *Stock Exchange Gazette*, moving to the *Financial Times* and then the *Daily Telegraph* as deputy City editor. After a spell as City editor of the *Guardian*, he rejoined the *Daily Telegraph* also as City editor. One day, while sitting in his office, Whittam Smith received a phone call from a reporter on *Business News* magazine asking him for a quote about Eddie Shah's launch of *Today*. Whittam Smith said he thought the venture a little foolhardy. Then, as he pondered the idea, he realized there was an opening for a new quality paper, particularly as *The Times* had recently been hit by industrial action. He confided in two *Telegraph* colleagues, Matthew Symonds and Stephen Glover. Together they decided to form a newspaper.

Whittam Smith went to the city and raised £18 million. By the end of 1986, the *Independent* newspaper was ready to launch, its name reflecting its policy of minority ownership. When the first issue appeared on 7 October 1986, the response was euphoric. Its design was classical, its writing erudite and its politics free-thinking. It also appealed to the new age of city yuppie. In the *Independent*'s first week, sales averaged 500,000 – 125,000 above its target – later settling on a figure of around 400,000. In 1987, Whittam Smith had the distinction of being voted Marketing Man of the Year by the Institute of Marketing and Journalist of the Year in the British Press Awards.

Under Whittam Smith's editorship, the *Independent* became a curious admixture of the highbrow and the trendy, recruiting big-name writers from *The Times* and *Sunday Times* and expanding its features into Living, Health and Technology sections. It was the sort of newspaper you could leave lying around to impress your friends. However, it was not quite established enough to gain the advertisers' unequivocal support, so during the recession it suffered more than its rivals. Then Whittam Smith made his first big mistake. He decided to start a Sunday version of the paper called the *Independent on Sunday*. His aim was a spoiling operation to squeeze out the newly formed *Sunday Correspondent*. In this he succeeded but at considerable cost to himself and Newspaper Publishing plc.

By 1991, both *Independent*s were losing money. To try to recoup his losses, Whittam Smith approached the owners of two European newspapers who put money into the papers and became shareholders. But the losses continued. Whittam Smith and his directors had clearly over-reached themselves. Newspaper Publishing looked around for backers. Then, in 1994, Mirror Group Newspapers bought a 28 per cent holding in the two papers. Whittam Smith resigned as editor and became chairman, selling most of his shares in the company.

The tale of the two *Independent*s is a cautionary one of an individual trying to do too much in an aggressively cut-throat market. The future of the two newspapers still remains uncertain as they continue to cut staff and resources in relentless cost-cutting exercises.

Sir David English's first job was as a cub reporter on the *Christchurch Times* in Hampshire. He then spent two years on the *Portsmouth Evening News* before joining the *Daily Mirror* as a reporter at the age of 20. After working as a foreign correspondent, English became associate editor of the *Daily Express* and editor of the *Daily Sketch*, moving to the *Mail*'s editorship when the two papers merged in 1971. The *Daily Mail* was a broadsheet with a daily circulation of 1.8 million, while its rival, the *Daily Express*, was selling 3.5 million copies a day. In a direct assault on their rival, English and his proprietor Lord Rothermere changed the *Daily Mail* into a smaller, more compact tabloid. The alchemy worked. The *Daily Mail* closed the gap on its rival and in five years the *Daily Express*'s circulation fell to 2.6 million, while the smaller *Mail*'s rose to 2 million.

With shrewd sense of purpose, English aimed the paper at the middle-market executive and the new working woman. He expanded the features section, recruiting such Fleet Street writers as Anne Leslie, Lynda Lee-Potter and John Edwards, and introduced lively right-wing commentaries. He also started a woman's section, with a faint whiff of feminism, catering for the latest health fads and high-street fashions. The *Daily Mail*'s advertisers reacted favourably.

From 1982 to 1983, English acted as editor-in-chief of the new *Mail on Sunday*, also targeted at a middle-class readership. He continued to edit the *Daily Mail* until 1992 when he became chairman and editor-in-chief of Associated Newspapers, the

Daily Mail's parent company. That year, the *Daily Mail*'s circulation was 1.7 million – compared to the *Daily Express*'s 1.54 million. It was an impressive figure in a slightly shrinking newspaper market, some former readers opting for the instant news coverage of cable and satellite television. Since then, the *Daily Mail*'s circulation has grown steadily to more than 1.8 million. The English–Rothermere axis has proved to be one of the news media's outstanding success stories.

David Montgomery is the typical cool, unflappable newspaperman. A colleague once said of him: 'He is the only guy I've ever known who can walk into a room and reduce the temperature by 10 degrees.' Educated at Bangor Grammar School, Montgomery, nickname Monty, went to Queen's University, Belfast, leaving with a degree in politics and history. He joined the *Daily Mirror* as a sub in Manchester before moving to the paper's London office and rising to deputy chief sub-editor. After a spell as chief sub of the *Sun*, Monty became assistant editor of the *People* (or *Sunday People* as it was then known) and, at the age of 37, editor of the *News of the World*, where he was renowned for scoops and catchy headlines.

Two years later, Monty became the second editor of *Today*. He told his first editorial conference that he was aiming the paper at 'greedy people'. He also concentrated on green issues, to appeal to a more liberal-minded element. By 1989, Monty had doubled *Today*'s circulation from 300,000 to 600,000, and to preserve his readership, he sometimes used stories that had appeared two or three days beforehand in other newspapers. If the *Sun* ran a feature about husband-swapping in Lewisham, *Today* would do likewise. If the *Daily Mirror* decided to serialize the life and loves of an eccentric pop star, Monty would produce his own in-house version. Soon he had a new nickname: the Jackdaw of Fleet Street. Sometimes, he even used the byline Jack Daw on *Today* stories. The *Daily Express* successfully sued Monty and *Today* for using quotes from an interview with Pamella Bordes, the controversial House of Commons researcher. Then, in a final twist of irony, *Today* sued and won damages from the *Daily Star* for lifting quotes from Princess Alexandra's daughter, Marina Ogilvy. After that, the Jackdaw went to roost.

In 1991, *Today*'s circulation began to flag. To help the newspaper cut its losses, Monty laid off 45 journalists. The decline continued and Andrew Knight, chairman of Rupert Murdoch's News International, *Today*'s parent company, moved Monty from his job into a relatively obscure executive post in Hong Kong. Though he had failed to maintain his early momentum on the newspaper, Monty had prevented *Today* from becoming yesterday's paper.

Soon afterwards he came back to Britain and started his own satellite TV company, London Live Television. After the death of Robert Maxwell, Monty was appointed chief executive of Mirror Group Newspapers. One of his first acts was to sack just over 100 casual journalists from the *Daily Mirror* and appoint new editors at the *Daily Mirror, Sunday Mirror* and the *People*. Recently, the ever-striving Monty's Mirror Group took control of the *Independent* and *Independent on Sunday*.

One more editor needs a mention. Peter Preston was editor of the *Guardian* from 1975 until early 1995 when he became editor-in-chief of the *Guardian* and its new sister paper, the *Observer*. It was a distinguished editorship in which he successfully fended off the threat of the *Independent* and helped revamp the paper into a more imaginative format. There was one blemish in his career – the sending of a cod fax, supposedly written on House of Commons notepaper by Jonathan Aitken MP, chief secretary to the Treasury, about a bill for a stay at the Ritz Hotel in Paris. It was a case of forgery in the furtherance of a story. Preston's reputation was further dented when soon afterwards it was revealed that, unknown to him, his features editor Richard Gott had received payments from the KGB. However neither of these incidents detracted from Preston's position as an outstanding figure in quality journalism.

An editor is a powerful figure. He is an opinion-maker whose columns can sway governments and influence millions of people. He often sees himself as a guardian of democracy and a protector of free speech. Sometimes an editor has to answer to the demands of greedy owners and the pressures of cash and circulation. Suddenly he becomes a cynical survivor, abusing his role and undermining the very people and public institutions he claims to serve. Let us hope today's editors respect their positions of power and do not become a greater threat to British democracy than those they so freely condemn.

4

Money Talks

'Information is only a commodity – like bread. It's the value of an individual's information to a commercial organization. We sell it, so why shouldn't they?'

Brian Hitchen

Newspaper offices used to hum with excitement when a scoop was brought in by a reporter or team of reporters. Each facet of the story was dissected in minute detail before being taken to the news editor who consulted with the editor and production department over the best way to present it.

Newspapers now have a more sober and calculating way of getting hold of stories – paying for them. This is popularly known as cheque-book journalism and involves complex negotiations and a contract signed by the newspaper and the person or persons being bought. Newspapers have always paid for information. In 1887, *The Times* had to pay £250,000 in libel fees and costs when it bought two letters said to have been written by the Irish MP Charles Parnell supporting the infamous Phoenix Park Murders. In the 1920s, newspapers sometimes footed defendants' legal bills at murder trials in return for exclusive stories. Even in the 1930s, newspapers paid for exclusives on the high seas or in the bars of seedy hotels. Buying stories has always been an accepted Fleet Street practice, but never on the scale of the 1990s.

The popular tabloids are Fleet Street's cheque-book specialists. Their favourite sources are the friends and relatives of potential victims, which may involve weeks of bartering before they agree to 'talk'. The promise of money can turn a small rumour into a full-blooded tale of sleaze and sensation. The precise figure depends on the story's saleability, the source's bargaining power and the newspaper buying the story. Insurance broker Samantha Phillips, who blamed sexism and sexual harassment for her sacking from City brokers Willis Corroon in 1994, sold her story to the *Daily Mail* for £5,000; Karen and Roger Humphries, whose baby Abbie was stolen by a woman posing as a hospital nurse received 20 pages of coverage in the *Daily Mirror* and a fee of £150,000.

Celebrities and members of the public have been fed so much scandal in the past ten years that they have become wilier in their negotiations with newspapers. Knowing the value of their information they will use publicity agents or middlemen to negotiate for them. The bargaining then turns into a Dutch auction as each side seeks to outwit the other before agreeing a final figure. However there is another, sadder side to the selling of sleaze. Sometimes when a tabloid reporter phones and asks for details of a potential story, the source, lured on by that elusive 15 minutes of fame, will say too much just because he knows his name is going to appear in the papers the next day. He may also fall prey to the reporter's cunning line of questioning as he delves for an angle and end up signing a contract he later regrets. The publicity may cause him to be shunned by friends and family and to suffer the humiliations of press exposure for years to come.

Vying for a story can involve high-speed air, sea or car chases between rival newspapers, secret bargaining between teams of solicitors and cunning scheming to outwit the opposition. As in all realms of commerce, media auctions have their own tricks of the trade. Sometimes, when several newspapers are bidding for the same story, one of them will suddenly increase the bidding by a substantial sum and arrange to meet the by now elated source. At the meeting, the newspaper's negotiator will write out a contract agreeing to make an immediate down payment of, say, ten per cent, pledging to pay the rest when the story is serialized. Though the story duly appears in the newspaper, the serialization may not go ahead. As a result the unfortunate source not only finds he is considerably out of pocket, but cannot sue as his contract states that the rest of his money is to be paid on publication of the serialization. There are several ways hapless members of the public can be taken in by slick negotiators, if they are not careful.

The subjects of buy-ups often have to face a hazardous grilling from the media. Victims of personal misfortune, for example, are often pounded with offers hours after disaster has struck. Such was the case of 51-year-old Jackie Greaves, a school secretary from Lancashire who with two fellow climbers slid into a deep gully in the Cairngorms. Her companions were rescued, but Miss Greaves spent two nights in sub-zero temperatures on an icy ledge before struggling through a blizzard and down the mountainside where she was fortunately found by a team of rescuers. She was flown to a nearby hospital suffering from hunger, dehydration and frostbite. During the night more than 20 journalists arrived and pestered hospital staff to let them speak to her. At first Miss Greaves refused then, reluctantly, she agreed to speak to the *Sun* who said they would pay her £40,000 if she would fly away in a private jet and give them an exclusive. Greaves turned down the offer as she was feeling too weak. Finally, after two hours of hard talking she agreed to give interviews at her bedside to the *Sun* and *Daily Mail*. The two newspapers paid her £20,000 apiece.

Another news media victim was the 22-year-old House of Commons researcher Emily Barr, who was said to have had an affair with her boss, Tory MP Hartley Booth. After the revelations appeared in the *Sunday Mirror*, the tabloids managed to cajole Miss Barr into selling her story as they said that the story of her 'affair' would be published anyway. They also told her that they had pictures of her appearing naked in life-drawing classes and knew she attended Socialist Workers' Party meetings while working for the Conservatives.

Even those who sell their stories willingly may later regret doing so. Such a decision may involve exposing and embarrassing friends, family and colleagues or lead to accusations of fortune-seeking. It might also create a lot of unwanted exposure, forcing the storyteller to move home, change his or her name by deed poll, or even leave the country altogether.

The quality newspapers and the middle-market tabloids occasionally publish disapproving leaders about the commercial methods of the popular tabloids, although they too are not immune from such activities. The *Sunday Times* titillated its readers with serializations of *Diana Her True Story*, by Andrew Morton, and *The Prince of Wales*, by Jonathan Dimbleby, while the *Daily Mail, Daily Express* and *Today* use both book serializations and story buy-ups about show-biz people, politicians' mistresses and more serious whodunnit-type tales. Serializations have even been tainted by spoiling operations. When the *Sunday Times* announced it was about to serialize Baroness Thatcher's memoirs, the *Daily Mirror* got hold of a copy of the manuscript three weeks before and printed their own extracts. The irony was that, instead of spoiling the *Sunday Times* serialization, it whetted the public's appetite and gave it an unexpected boost.

Cheque-book journalism is a tough market in which the news value of a story can change in 24 hours. A newspaper might buy a story one day for £5,000, or £25,000 if several other papers are bidding for it, and not publish the next day because something else bigger and more interesting has come up.

The man with the highest profile in the publicity market is the agent Max Clifford. He has earned his clients millions of pounds from kiss 'n tell stories. He told me: 'Selling newspapers stories about aggrieved mistresses is a game. The tabloids are using stories they would never have dared to print ten years ago. Journalists are told "If you don't go and dig up the dirt on this or that personality, you will be sacked". They no longer have the freedom to go after the stories they want to. Nowadays publicity agents like myself find it easier to sell stories, as many journalists are on the defensive and frightened of letting down powerful proprietors like Rupert Murdoch.'

Clifford's first big media deal was the 'Freddie Starr Ate My Hamster' story in 1986. After appearing in a show in Manchester, Starr stayed with friends in the city. Unable to find anything to eat, the comedian put their pet hamster between two slices of bread and jokingly pretended to take a bite. Next day, the story was picked up by a *Sun* reporter. Clifford, Starr's agent, immediately organized a photo-call of the comedian with a hamster on his shoulder and sold it to the *Sun*. It appeared on the paper's front page the next day, out-scooping the *Daily Mirror* and *Daily Star*, spawning a flurry of 'F S A M H' T-shirts and boosting Starr's slightly flagging career. Among other Clifford coups were the sale of photographs of the Princess of Wales exercising in an Isleworth gym, which earned the photographer–gym owner more than £1 million; marketing the career of the Twickenham rugby streaker Erica Roe and handling Pamella Bordes's newspaper publicity.

His biggest kiss 'n tell deals were the Alan Clark/Harkess girls scandal (which netted the Harkess family around £200,000), and the affair of Lady Bienvenida Buck and the unfortunate chief of defence staff Sir Peter Harding (which earned Lady Buck £175,000). He was also approached by the actress Antonia de Sancha after the first media reports of her affair with the Minister of Fun, National Heritage Secretary David Mellor. Clifford then handled all her newspaper and television interviews, putting a spin on stories about the couples' love-making and bedtime habits, all of which Mellor has emphatically denied. It earned her approximately £100,000.

People who sell stories to the tabloids end up richer but not necessarily happier. Mistresses who try to get even with their lovers by printing revelations of their affairs often find the public has more sympathy for the victims they have betrayed. Lady Bienvenida Buck was snubbed by many of her high society friends when her story was published; and Captain James Hewitt was ostracized by his former officer friends, shunned by the public and found his social invitations had dwindled dramatically.

However money doesn't always talk. Newspapers sometimes end up having to pay the people they are writing about – in libel actions. During the 1980s and 1990s there have been several notable pay-outs to people who have successfully sued the news media. In 1995, Liverpool football club's former manager Graham Souness won £750,000 after a *People* article alleged he had behaved meanly to his former wife; the author and former politician Jeffery Archer was awarded £500,000 against the *Daily Star*; the actress and photographer Koo Stark has won more than £300,000 from ten successful libel actions against news-papers; while Sara Keays, the former mistress of ex-Conservative party chairman, Cecil Parkinson, has been awarded an estimated £200,000 from libel cases against the news media.

The problem is that the more the news media speculates, the greater the risks of libel. Recently, judges have been making considerable awards to libel victims to try and curb a press that sometimes lets its headline-attracting talents override its fact-checking abilities.

One of the media's main sources of stories is the agency. The leading agencies for British news are PA News (formerly the Press Association) and UK News, which cover most major events and happenings throughout the country. Their foreign equivalent is Reuters, whose correspondents cover many of today's overseas news events. Both PA News and Reuters have direct input to all the major newspapers and air-time programmes. There are also around 50 independent agencies covering the main news areas of Britain. Their job is to find stories for newspapers (as well as radio and television stations). They then sell them on, either as high-fee exclusives or to all the main national newspaper and media outlets. If a big story breaks, the local agency is often paid to cover it for the newspapers. A more humble version of the agency is the stringer, a journalist who works for a local newspaper and covers stories for the nationals on a casual basis, offering them tip-offs and, if necessary, acting as their local correspondent. A third category is the freelance. He is a hard-working journalist who writes stories on his own initiative and sells them on to the national newspapers, radio and television. A good freelance, who may be based anywhere from Peking to Peckham, has strong bargaining powers with newspapers and can earn considerable sums of money. Newspapers sometimes pay freelances a retainer for their services, or else use them on a more casual, shift-work basis. In 1994, the *Sun* paid its agency and freelance journalists £8 million for stories and tip offs.

Like the police, newspapers have their own informants. These range from police insiders and industrial spies to ordinary members of the public. Such an informant leaked the stories of the Princess of Wales's telephone calls to her friend Oliver Hoare, which at the time was blamed on a British Telecom employee. The story nearly didn't make the front pages at all. The first version, written by John Twomey of the *Daily Express*, was spiked because of its sensational nature. The tragic 1994 tale of MP Stephen Milligan's suicide in the kitchen of his Hammersmith home could only have come from an informant with close links with the police force.

Many good stories stem from reporters' contacts with chauffeurs, taxi-drivers, airport staff, barmen and hairdressers – in fact anyone they are likely to meet in their favourite haunts. Useful tit-bits such as a well-known celebrity's ex-directory telephone number, the time of a flight booking or a random snippet of gossip can earn fees of around £100 a time. Other tip-offs come from members of the public, or witnesses of events just after they have occurred. A mega-story such as the discovery of love letters written by a member of the royal family could command a fee of up to £500,000.

In recent years Fleet Street reporters have found themselves on the receiving end of another type of story – the hoax. With higher costs and more pages to fill, newspaper reporters and executives sometimes find they are struggling to find stories. This makes the job of the newspaper hoaxer even easier when he is trying to convince reporters and news desks of a story's validity.

One of the most famous hoaxers of the British news media is a former RAF pilot called Joe Flynn. Flynn has duped the media, the government, several embassies and the CIA more than 20 times since the mid-1970s. Sometimes known as Joe 'The Sting' Flynn, his biggest hoax was when he persuaded the Pulitzer Prize-winning journalist Seymour Hersh that Robert Maxwell and his *Daily Mirror* foreign editor Nick Davies were involved in selling arms and had organized a plot with Israeli intelligence to kidnap Mordechai Vanunu, a nuclear technician who had leaked Israeli weapon secrets.

Flynn telephoned both Hersh and his publisher Matthew Evans, chairman of Faber and Faber, saying he was a private detective called Patrick Begg with crucial information about the alleged plot. Evans paid him £500 for the story. Later, Flynn telephoned Hersh again and said he had videos and tapes of telephone conversations to back up his evidence against Maxwell and Davies. He was sent two more cheques for £400 and £390. Because Fleet Street had heard rumours about Maxwell's alleged links with foreign intelligence networks, the story was highlighted in all the daily newspapers. A month later, Flynn telephoned Hersh and Evans and told them the story was a complete fabrication.

Flynn's first newspaper hoax occurred in 1976 when he told the news desk of Rupert Murdoch's *New York Star* that he had acquired the death shoes of Jimmy Hoffa, the recently murdered leader of an American trade union. He arranged to meet a *Star* reporter and produced his evidence: a pair of scuffed brown leather shoes that, unknown to the reporter, he had bought in a junk shop. Flynn was paid £30,000. Again he telephoned the newspaper and boastfully pointed out that they had been duped.

Flynn uses a variety of disguises ranging from a black handlebar moustache to a long, red hippy-style wig. Sometimes he meets reporters at airports and railway stations using such aliases as Lee Paul Carpinter, Rocco Salvatore, Edward Gray and Harry Banks. So effective is Flynn's deception that though Fleet Street journalists sometimes suspect he is misleading them, they can never actually prove it.

The conman's cleverest sleight of pen was a story he sold to the *News of the World* in 1981. He telephoned the Sunday newspaper and said the Libyan leader Colonel Gaddafi was recruiting British-based West Indians to Libya, training them as shoot-to-kill hit-men and sending them back to Britain again. Posing as arms dealer Edward Christian, Flynn persuaded *News of the World* reporter Gerry Brown and photographer Ian Cutler to meet him in Rome. During three weeks of negotiations, the newspaper paid him £3,000, publishing a story headlined: 'Libya Trains Britons to Kill on Our Streets.' Flynn later extracted £1,500 from the *People* for a similar story. On another occasion he persuaded the *Independent*'s salesroom correspondent, Geraldine Norman, to pay him £250 for supplying false information about thefts from the California-based John Paul Getty museum.

Another conman called Rocky Ryan has carried out a number of memorable Fleet-Street hoaxes. He leaked supposed details of secret meetings between Prince Charles and the Princess of Wales when they were trying to patch up their marriage. He has also reported numerous sightings of Lord Lucan in different parts of the world. In 1993, Ryan telephoned the *Sun* posing as a Buckingham Palace security official and said he had been warned that a group of homosexual serial killers was about to break into the palace. The next day the newspaper ran the headline: 'Palace Gays in Murder Alert.'

I met another clever hoaxer when I was a news agency reporter in Maidstone, Kent. A small, dapper individual with silver hair and a little black moustache, he travelled the country opening model agencies, taking high fees from potential models and inviting the local news media to photograph them for the next day's newspapers. Before the models were able to get any work, he had donned a new disguise and disappeared with their fees to the next town. Eventually his frauds caught up with him and he was committed and jailed for five years. After the court case, he admitted using more than 20 different disguises to fool journalists.

One of the biggest spoofs of recent times was the Hitler Diaries serialization that was bought by the *Sunday Times*. The fake diaries were originally sold to Germany's *Stern* magazine for £2.5 million by three German businessmen in 1983. Before deciding whether to buy the story, the *Sunday Times* asked the Oxford historian Sir Hugh Trevor-Roper (now Lord Dacre) to confirm the diaries' authenticity. Trevor-Roper, a director of *The Times* and the author of *The Last Days of Hitler*, said he believed they were genuine. So the *Sunday Times* went ahead and paid £250,000 for the serialization before realizing they had been duped.

There is a further, more subtle form of news media manipulation. Public relations is a by-product of modern commercial practice, a sophisticated method of getting an item, service or cause into the public eye. Most large companies and public bodies employ press officers or public relations companies to pass information on to, and sometimes mislead, the news media.

Top PROs such as Sir Tim Bell, Mrs Thatcher's former adviser, and Lynne Franks, who has promoted such causes as Amnesty International, Greenpeace and the Variety Club of Great Britain in the 1980s and 1990s, use their persuasive powers to turn simple ideas into national issues. Sometimes they are referred to as spin-doctors for their ability to put a spin, or new angle, on a story to keep it running in the news media.

The PRO's methods of getting valuable air-time and column inches may range from entertaining journalists to lunches and dinners at expensive restaurants, buying air tickets for exotic family holidays, or handing over gifts such as televisions, hi-fis and cars. Some journalists are strong-minded enough to resist such blatant examples of media payola; others are loath to bite the hand that feeds them.

The PROs' job is to present their companies in as favourable a light as possible. Behind a PRO's smooth façade may be such vested interests as boosting his or her company's share prices, business expansion, fending off competitive companies, covering up a scandal they do not wish to be made public, a possible breach of national security or a secret deal they wish to hide from their rivals.

The PRO's favourite method of passing on information is the press release. This is an item of commercial news printed on headed notepaper that is sent, with a covering letter, to the news desks of the national or local media. Press releases are usually verbose and over-technical. The point they are making is often lost in the telling. The result is that most are either rewritten or thrown away. Occasionally, a release with genuine news content will catch the news editor's eye and a reporter will be ordered to follow the story up.

A more stylish PR technique is the press conference. This is used to announce a big company event such as an impending takeover, a new product or a technical breakthrough. The press conference is usually hosted by the company's chairman or chief executive and includes a panel of experts who will answer questions put by the assembled journalists. The idea is to make the company look professional and inspire confidence. Often the more experts present, the less professional the company. One of the cannier ways PROs get their messages across at press conferences is by handing round glossy brochures. They also use endless statistics, data and information to give a glowing and confident impression of the company's achievements. Naturally every self-respecting PRO fears the clever journalist who asks one tricky question too many.

A smart PRO may decide to use another, less straightforward, form of persuasion – the press reception. This is usually held in a plush hotel banqueting suite so as to invoke an air of glamour and sophistication. The aim of the reception is to lull journalists into a light-hearted and uncaring mood with large quantities of wine, canapés, little gift-wrapped souvenirs and occasionally slim, gift-wrapped waitresses. Teams of PROs and young assistants mingle with journalists and try to sweet-talk them into giving favourable write-ups about the company and its affairs. Such largesse may be just a slick attempt to cover up a potential company scandal or to prevent a fall in share prices. It is arguable whether the average press reception succeeds. Most journalists view them as irrelevant two-hour freebies in a busy day – no more, no less.

PRO's – once described by the *Sunday Telegraph* as the Agents of Mumbo Jumbo – often have a high regard for their trade. A booklet titled *All You Need To Know About PR* issued by the Public Relations Consultants Association says: 'Some journalists claim to dislike some PR people, but this is to be expected in any close relationship. In reality, many journalists rely on PR people as a source of many – if not most – of their stories.' It would be interesting to see if the majority of Fleet Street editors share this view.

A popular Fleet-Street freebie is the free holiday. Travel companies pay for journalists to go on such trips as a two-week package in Spain or a safari in Africa in return for a free mention or write-up in their newspapers. Another media sweetener is the press trip. These can range from flights to New York on Concorde and visits to faraway places to more local freebies like a day at a French trout farm or a weekend in Rome. To celebrate the 50th anniversary of D-Day in 1994, the British and French Ministries of Defence arranged for a fleet of landing-craft to disgorge an invading band of queasy journalists on to the beaches of Dunkirk.

Political PR is a more specialist domain. Some firms are so keen to get parliamentary – and indirectly media – coverage of their interests and products that they use a number of London-based firms of lobbyists to bring issues to the attention of MPs. Parliamentary PR became a more controversial issue recently when the *Sunday Times* revealed that three MPs had been paid sums of up to £1,000 each to ask questions in the House of Commons.

All political parties and government ministries pay teams of press officers to pass on information to the media. One particularly effective source of PR is the parliamentary lobby briefing in which the prime minister, ministers and MPs give 'off-the-record' stories to a select group of journalists. Margaret Thatcher sometimes used Number 10 lobby briefings to discredit colleagues who had fallen out of favour with her. When Nigel Lawson resigned as chancellor of the exchequer after publicly disagreeing with Mrs Thatcher's economic adviser Alan Walters, her press officer Bernard Ingham criticized Lawson at a lobby briefing. Lawson referred to the attack as 'black propaganda'. Former leader of the House of Commons, Norman St John Stevas, who received similar treatment at a journalists' briefing, said he had become a victim of the Ingham Effect.

The work of the political PRO is particularly feverish at election time. Not only does he have to arrange daily press conferences and press statements, but also answer a hotline of telephone queries from members of the public. These can range from the party's latest policies to the colour of its leader's shirts. Many PROs go on to stand as parliamentary candidates themselves. One notable example is the Labour front-bencher Gerald Kaufman, who spent several years at No 10 Downing Street as Harold Wilson's chief press officer.

However the canniest source of political propaganda is the leak. The first two years of Mrs Thatcher's prime ministership were acknowledged as the leakiest in history, one Conservative backbencher pointing out: 'The House of Commons was like a sieve. The country had a two-tier administration – government by the media and government by mediocrities.' Because of their unofficial status, leaks can backfire. The Labour leader Harold Wilson once told Robert Carvel, the London *Evening Standard*'s political editor, he was about to sack a cabinet minister. Carvel printed the story. The next day, Wilson changed his mind.

One of the reasons for the leak's impact is the anonymity of the civil service. Under the 1889 and 1911 Official Secrets

Acts, government officials are not allowed to disclose information to journalists unless they have received official permission to do so. Thus leaks enable journalists to get stories from the heart of government. They also enable the government to sell on vote-winning propaganda and use cunning cover-ups for the real workings of government.

People and institutions who manipulate the news media are playing journalists at their own game, often using such favourite media techniques as misleading information, clever disguises, cod faxes and money to do so. Sometimes it is very difficult to tell who is conning whom. Journalists mislead their quarries into giving them stories, while their exploiters sell on propaganda disguised as stories. In a daily battle of wits in which both sides think they have the upper hand, the news media probably has a higher integrity rating than its manipulators. It remains to be seen how long it takes for current events to change all that. The sad fact is that whoever wins, truth will always be the main casualty.

5

Keep Taking the Tabloids

'We haven't had a libel writ in a week. And what
we've got is a bloody awful newspaper.'

Kelvin MacKenzie

If an alien from another planet was asked to name Britain's
seven deadly sins he would probably say drugs, football
hooliganism, rape, fraud, child abuse, class prejudice ... and the
tabloids. Today's tabloid newspapers represent the ugly side of
British life and like to feature all the other imponderables in
glaring Technicolor or stark black and white. On some days,
the average tabloid can look more like a lurid horror comic
than a newspaper; on others, you could be forgiven for
mistaking one of them for a flimsy version of a men's magazine.
Brash, vulgar and sensational, you would never find a tabloid
perched on a silver breakfast tray ready for some informed
reading or waiting to greet the customers in the foyer of a
respectable hotel. It is more likely to be found scattered among

63

the toast and cereals on the breakfast table or stuffed
into somebody's back pocket on his daily journey to work.
Written in bold, punchy prose with eye-catching photographs and clamorous headings, the tabloid panders to the
emotions of its audience and won't try to impress them with
long-winded phrases and analyses of events or a day in
parliament.

The tabloids are Britain's merchants of sleaze. They have
created a climate of bad taste and disgust, one minute
highlighting the worst features of British society, the next
judging and deriding public figures before disgorging them on
to an increasingly cynical British public. It is a climate they
preserve to whet the public's appetite. They print regardless of
whether their readers wish to read tales that 15 years ago
they would never dare repeat to their parents, let alone
children.

Each day we hear about a new trial by tabloid, as another
politician, pop star, film star, footballer or football manager
falls from grace. Often the celebrity was brought to public
notice by the newspaper itself. Now he or she has to suffer the
indignity of seeing his or her private life and supposed
indiscretions exposed to several million readers. Sometimes, the
media's victims bring the sleaze on themselves through
misdemeanour or attention seeking, but they do not deserve
the constant stream of vilification and speculation that
follows. Time and again, we hear the refrain: 'My life has been
ruined by the media' or 'I lost my job because of the news
media'.

People in the public eye are becoming increasingly defensive
when dealing with the press, sometimes using public relations
officers and spokesmen to put their messages across. Sadly,
such tactical manoeuvres only make the tabloids more
suspicious and intrusive and often lead to greater speculation.
Sometimes the victim blames the PRO, but usually he has been
coaxed into a corner from which not even the most astute team
of PROs can prise him. Media intrusion has become a
dangerous and vicious circle.

In the 1960s, tabloids were bright, brash, vulgar, but relatively harmless; in the 1970s, they became sharper and more sensational, using their media influence to spread gossip and taunt the famous; in the 1980s and 1990s, they turned into brazen, anti-establishment scandal sheets, not only pillorying public figures and royalty but undermining many of the institutions and traditions the British respect and hold dear. The pioneer of the new journalism was Kelvin MacKenzie's *Sun*.

MacKenzie took over the *Sun*'s editorship in 1981, replacing a dynamic Yorkshireman called Larry Lamb. Lamb had laid the foundations of the modern tabloid with Page Three Girls and provocative prose. Then, with the determination of a German Panzer division, Macca bullied and cajoled his *Sun* employees into producing a work of shock, horror and sleaze. Any story that did not titillate the reader had to be rewritten. It did not matter if some of it was untrue. When I worked on the *Sun*, I remember being asked to insert different names and places in a story about a woman who had left her husband to prevent any risk of libel.

Macca edited by fear, shouting and swearing at his employees, sacking a sub-editor who dared to change one of his headlines and showing the door to another who swore back at him. He was a brilliant technician, with a flair for eye-catching pages and attention-grabbing headings. He also had an instinctive grasp of his audience, their needs and attitudes, likes and dislikes.

Under Macca, the *Sun*'s circulation soared to more than four million. It was condemned in the House of Commons for its crudeness and hated – though sometimes grudgingly admired – by its rivals. Year after year, the other Fleet Street populars tried to emulate the manic Macca formula. But, hard as they struggled, they never even managed to approach it. The *Daily Star* introduced its own version of the Page Three Girl known as the Star-bird, but for some reason its models often looked a little tawdry compared with the *Sun*'s. Then the *Daily Mirror*, which was recognized as Britain's leading tabloid newspaper in the 1960s and 1970s, made a classic strategic error when Robert Maxwell banned all topless models from its pages. It was a policy that was destined to fail.

With its unique brand of journalism, the *Sun* became the archetype of the modern tabloid. It is a style that defies ethical standards and respect for people's feelings. Responsible public opinion now rues the lines of Tom Stoppard's play *Night and Day*: 'Junk journalism is the evidence of a society that has got at least one thing right, that there should be nobody with the power to dictate where responsible journalism begins.' But where does tabloid journalism begin? Serious commentators and thinkers are calling for an end to the tyranny of the fourth-rate estate.

Macca's editorship continued through the 1980s into the 1990s. By then, the newspaper resembled a catalogue of sleaze, sex, black humour and mutant labels as he tried to parody the prejudices of the man-in-the-street. Every day a new one would spring on to its pages. Poofters, blacks, all foreigners including Froggies (Frenchmen), Argies (Argentinians) and Scipies (Mexicans), trade unionists, skinheads, peace activists, prostitutes and any member of the establishment who had been having a hard time. All became victims of the Macca menagerie.

The formula was clever and calculated. MacKenzie had worked as a reporter on local newspapers in deprived areas of east London and believed he knew his readers' favourite topics. Each day he gave them a predictable blend of birds, booze, baccy, betting and bingo as well as raunchy stories about personalities, TV soaps, drugs, bed and bawd, sport and crime, and large doses of scandal and gossip to put spice into their lives.

Macca was also selective. Knowing the commercial clout of his advertisers, he didn't wish to antagonize them. So he rarely ran stories about 18-stone Mabel from Maidenhead indulging in marathon chocolate binges (several well-known confectioners advertised in the *Sun*), or the dentist from Doncaster who ruined his teeth after drinking too many Cokes (another lucrative advertiser). Cash and circulation ruled.

Macca, a former public schoolboy, even behaved like his idea of a typical *Sun* reader, dropping his hs, talking in an east London accent and yelling 'bollocks' if anyone tried to reason with him. I can even remember him falling off his chair during a heated exchange over a splash headline. He would stomp round the office brandishing his green felt-tip pen like a headmaster with his cane. If a phrase annoyed him he would strike it out and yell 'that's crap', bellow at a hapless sub to put more sex into a reader's letter then, with a flash of devilish wit, insert his own witty headline such as 'Sex-mad soldier gets the bullet'. Occasionally his headlines went over the top. When the word 'Gotcha' appeared above the story of the sinking of the *Belgrano* in the Falklands War, Macca was given a stern lecture by his proprietor, Rupert Murdoch, for its tastelessness. It also managed to create a major diplomatic row. The headline was wisely dropped from the newspaper's later editions.

Macca used many familiar journalistic tricks to stay ahead of his rivals. Newspaper moles would alert him of splashes due to appear in other papers. Sometimes he sent journalists across Fleet Street to pinch pictures from the *Daily Express*'s library or, disguising himself as a *Daily Mirror* news editor, telephone the *Mirror*'s stone-sub (the man who checks the final proofs) to find out the paper's main stories of the day.

Somewhat paradoxically, the *Sun* editor was a disciplinarian. He once told his reporters: 'I am disgusted at the length of your lunch hours. Two-hour breaks do not do this newspaper, the country, or yourselves a favour. It is no wonder that Britain is rapidly turning into a Third World nation, if, when we arrive at work, we do anything but work.' When he was angry with a member of staff he would summon him or her to his office and say: 'Don't speak. Take your bollocking – then fuck off.' But there was method behind his sternness. Creating an intense atmosphere kept employees' nerves on a knife-edge and sharpened their approach to their work. As a result, the

Sun sparkled. Murdoch's view was: 'MacKenzie is ...
screaming and shouting, and he's good. Somehow it works.'
One reporter described a day at the *Sun* as like being in the
middle of a siege.

In the 1990s, the *Sun* assumed an ugly side. Macca and his
senior staffmen began to use stories that undermined the royal
family and public figures. One was a middle-page photo spread
of a five-months' pregnant Princess Di wearing a skimpy bikini
in the Caribbean, which certainly shook the *Sun*'s royalist
readers. Each Monday at the morning news conference,
reporters and photographers were ordered to systematically
pursue members of the royal family and produce sensational
stories about them.

The Queen sued over one royal story – a leaked photograph
of Princess Bea, the Duchess of York's daughter. The photo was
to have been used as part of a family portrait on the Queen's
annual Christmas card, a tradition the Queen takes very
seriously, often using royal photographers such as Lord
Snowdon and Norman Parkinson. When the photograph
appeared in the *Sun* with the heading 'The Queen Bea', the
Queen's lawyers wrote to the paper threatening breach of
copyright if it was used again.

The next day the *Sun* ran a story headed: 'HRH is not
amused – you cheeky Beas' with a miniature copy of the
photograph and the caption: 'The magical photo touched the
nation with its charm and warmth. But the Queen was not
amused to see it.' The Queen took Macca and the *Sun* to court
for breach of copyright and won, the *Sun* agreeing to pay
£100,000 to four of the Queen's favourite charities. The origin
of the photograph was a story in itself. It had been sold to the
paper by a schoolgirl who spent her summer holidays working
in a south London photographic laboratory.

Public figures soon found themselves on the receiving end of
the *Sun*'s sensation-seeking stories. Judges were a popular, if
easy, target. Judge Martin Bowley, of the south-eastern circuit,
was forced to resign after the *Sun* alleged he had had a

homosexual affair. The *Sun* even started a Trial by Press, inviting readers to send in their verdicts on recent sentences handed out by judges. In some ways it was an honourable cause, as there had been many cases of excessive leniency over rape trials, with extremely harsh sentences passed for relatively minor offences. Yet the main reason for the paper's sudden preoccupation with justice was less honourable – higher readership figures.

One of the *Sun*'s most unfortunate victims was Sir Ralph Halpern, chairman of Burton the tailor, who was alleged to have had five-times-a-night bonking sessions with a 19-year-old photographic model called Fiona Wright. In an analogy to a well-known fruit, Macca's *Sun* used the headline: 'Fyffe Times a Night'.

In their efforts to sustain circulation, the *Sun*'s rivals followed its example. One public figure after another was toppled into a cauldron of sleaze. It seemed as if nothing, and no one, was sacred.

Today's tabloids often forget, or choose to ignore, the press's role as Britain's leading watchdog and arbiter of good public behaviour. By the very nature of their roles, all public servants and celebrities should be accountable for their actions through the news media. But they should not have to be used as targets by mischief-making 'investigative' reporters and newspaper executives.

Tabloid editors are only too aware that scandals and gossip boost their newspapers' circulations. The problem is that their excesses go unchecked and they can get away with almost anything. It means that an editor such as Wendy Henry, then of the *News of the World*, was able to send her reporters out for ten months, dogging the footsteps of television newscaster Frank Bough while the newspaper ran a succession of stories about the newscaster's alleged visits to London massage parlours and cocaine-snorting parties. The adverse publicity led to Bough being dropped as a presenter from two important BBC television programmes. It took more than a year for him to reappear on the air and wrest back some of his former reputation.

Another victim was television interviewer Russell Harty, who was said to have had massage and smacking sessions with an Earls Court rent-boy. The Harty story, which appeared on and off for more than a year, was one of the ugliest examples of media intrusion. When Harty was admitted to St James's Hospital, Leeds, with Hepatitis B, two tabloid reporters posing as doctors visited his bedside, recording details of his notes and conversations between doctors and nurses about his condition, and snatching pictures of the broadcaster with a secret camera. Harty eventually died of a combination of hepatitis and exhaustion.

The most blatant example of tabloid fantasy is the *Sunday Sport*. It was founded in 1986 by David Sullivan, a former London university graduate who spent 71 days in Wormwood Scrubs for living off immoral earnings. The *Sunday Sport*, which later appeared on weekdays as the *Daily Sport*, is more like a men's magazine than a daily paper, featuring photos of nude models and soft-porn centre spreads – a nudespaper rather than a newspaper. It carries lively sports coverage, but news items are rare. Most of its stories are based on science fiction, such as the Second World War bomber said to have been found on the moon, or the Martians that had their wicked way with three Basildon housewives. One favourite was a picture of Jimmy Wrinkle, a man who slimmed down from 52 to 12 stone and was frequently pictured in all his crinkled glory. Another story the *Sport* likes to repeat is that Elvis Presley is still alive. Sightings have been reported all over the USA and Britain, and several women have claimed to have had affairs with him. The campaign has also spawned a flurry of Elvis look-alikes, mementoes and literature.

The *Sunday* and *Daily Sport*s do make occasional concessions to news. But if they find nothing sensational enough has happened in the previous 24 hours, the news editor sometimes instructs six or seven reporters to go into a private room for the afternoon and concoct stories zany and outrageous enough to titillate their readers. The *Sports'* philosophy seems to be very simple. Make the breasts bigger and the stories more outlandish and you attract a greater readership. However their circulation figures do not reflect this. Most of the time they sell around 200,000 copies a day (compared with 4 million plus for the *Sun*) and lose money. Many of those who buy the *Sports* are regular readers of another daily newspaper, secretly slipping one into their briefcase when their wives, girlfriends or office colleagues aren't looking, or else hiding it in their copy of *The Times* or *Daily Telegraph*. The only overseas equivalents are the USA's supermarket tabloids, the *National Enquirer* and the *Star*.

In the late 1980s, the circulations of the middle-market tabloids began to suffer from the tawdry scandals that stared out from the news-stands and hoardings. So they reverted to a more intrusive and investigative style of journalism. The difference was that their stories were more straightforward, lacking the rabble-rousing fervour and spicy tittle-tattle of the popular tabloids; also their targets tended to be more respectable, their behaviour less shocking. Middle-class actors with failed marriages and film stars with undeclared mistresses were the standard fare, while the misdemeanours of royals and politicians received slightly more detached coverage than the populars saw fit to give them. At first the quality broadsheets were content to print admonitory leaders about the sensations of the nation, until they too saw the commercial value of sleaze, and started carrying detailed reports on their front and main news pages.

Sometimes, the popular tabloids carry stories with public interest elements, such as the government getting it wrong over Europe, the NHS being off colour, and the taxman mistakenly adding too many noughts to someone's tax returns. Human interest stories about the plight of single mothers or the miseries of being homeless and features about badly treated pets and the iniquities of hunting give them a much-needed touch of pathos, while a generous blend of sport, women's features and humour add to their entertainment value as Britain's most highly-read newspapers. But such innocent reporting remains supplementary to the daily conveyor belt of sex, scandal and sleaze.

In 1989, the tabloids went over the top. The event was the FA Cup semi-final between Liverpool and Nottingham Forest. The venue: Hillsborough football stadium, Sheffield. Before the game, the local police diverted a large section of the crowd through an extra gate manned by just one policeman. As the milling hoard tried to squeeze through, several barricades collapsed and fans started being trampled underfoot. The result was mayhem. Scuffles broke out between rival groups of fans and supporters were injured and killed. Fear and panic reigned.

The next day, the *Daily Mirror* carried ghoulish photographs of the dying and the dead. Then the *Sun* ran a blatant rabble-rousing story called The Truth. It accused Liverpool fans of being drunk, urinating on and beating up police officers and picking the pockets of dead victims. As Macca later admitted, much of the story was speculative with no named sources. The *Daily Star* too ran an exaggerated report of the tragedy with the tactless heading 'Dead Fans Robbed by Drunk Thugs'.

In their quest for readership, the three popular tabloids had painted an alarming and sinister picture of a national tragedy in which 95 football fans had died. The people of Liverpool were enraged. Newsagents banned both the *Sun* and the *Star*, thousands cancelled their daily orders for the two papers. The tabloids were openly challenged over their version of events by the city's evening paper, the *Liverpool Echo*. They had no defence. Even Fleet Street's most cynical veterans were shaken by the tabloids' behaviour. The *Sun*'s Liverpool sales dropped by just over 200,000 – from 524,000 to 320,000 copies a day. It took several years for Merseyside readers to start to forgive such an insensitive piece of journalism.

During the late 1980s and early 1990s, trouble of all kinds followed the *Sun*. When it carried a poorly researched exposé of Elton John in 1987, the pop star sued and won £1 million in libel damages. Week after week, libel threats, Press Council adjudications and angry letters poured into the newspaper's offices. In one year alone, the *Sun* received 50 writs. No one, whether sportsman, ballet dancer, ski instructor, circus manager, stand-up comic, wicker-chair repairer or country vicar was spared the *Sun*'s unrelenting exposure. Famous film stars such as Rock Hudson and David Niven were ghoulishly portrayed on their deathbeds; pictures of Aids victims, including film director Derek Jarman and actor Anthony Perkins, were featured in stories about the 'Gay Plague'; football hooligans, lager louts and skinheads were shown in all their unedifying ugliness, and readers could study the tawdry details of at least one bonking story a day.

Sometimes the tension was so high at the *Sun* that reporters and editors hurled abuse at one another and threw cups and ashtrays across the offices. On several occasions reporters wrestled away their frustration in the corridors. Macca worked a 14-hour day to keep the paper's circulation soaring. He also spent many hours on the telephone to Rupert Murdoch attempting to justify his choice of lead stories or splashes. Sub-editors worked 12-hour shifts, sometimes with only a 15-minute break, as they sharpened up the stories and headlines, polishing the newspaper until it shone. Reporters, diarists and feature writers dashed to and fro at Macca's bidding. One minute he would yell at a feature writer to put the phone down on a correspondent who was asking too much money; the next he would be ordering the Hollywood reporter to put more sleaze into a film-star exposé.

In 1994, Macca decided he had had enough of tabloid journalism, leaving the *Sun* to start a career in television. He went in style with a going-away party at Planet Hollywood, the West End restaurant, arranged by his friend, former *Sun* columnist Richard Littlejohn. Witty tributes were paid by colleagues, employees and former protegés. Then, to the cheering throng's delight, Macca picked up a microphone on a karaoke machine and sang: 'I did it my way'. It was a fitting epitaph for a 13-year reign of tabloid tyranny.

Pulitzer Prize-winner Jimmy Breslin describes the tabloids as newspapers 'designed for people leading dreadfully dull lives ... with a great formula – animal stories, axe murderers and the bird of the day'. Daily doses of sensation are like an addictive drug – to be taken at regular, two-hour intervals between each fix. Like any drug, titillation is a short-term remedy for boredom. It can also be an unhealthy one, over-exciting the reader and raising his or her blood pressure. Repeated fixes of violence, hooliganism and aggression can give the reader a warped and pessimistic view of the world. It may temporarily thrill, but it can also raise the anxiety level.

Newspaper owners and editors invariably under-rate the intelligence of their readers. Because of their newspapers' high circulations they assume their readers enjoy daily extracts of sleaze and revelation. It is time they raised their standards. In an information-led society, many people like to read factual news items and serious commentary as well as lighter, gossipy-style stories in their popular newspapers. There is nothing wrong with the odd sexy picture or scene of violence. But newspapers need balance and variety.

At present, the tabloids have a dangerous hold over their readers. Members of the public tend to believe what they read in them and, for the past five years, have been lulled into a fantasy world of sensationalism and prurience. Editors know seedy stories about personalities are relatively easy to research and sell to their readers, while on the more lurid tabloids, reporters have been known to embellish stories or make them up if they cannot find anything else to put into their columns.

Modern owners and editors must give readers what they deserve. They must raise the tone of their stories and lower the temperature of their newspapers. We do not want our tabloids to turn into the muck-raking and mind-bending monstrosities of the USA.

6

The Royal Picture Show

'A celebrity is a person who works hard all his life to become well known, and then wears dark glasses to avoid being recognized.'

Fred Allen, journalist and author

The lure of fame turns bit-part actors into film stars, handymen into war heroes and criminals into best-selling authors. Few achieve it, and those who do usually make it through a unique blend of talent, hard work, luck and courage. Recently fame has taken on a hollow ring. It no longer has the elusive aura it used to; neither is it trendy to praise people or to put them on a pedestal for their achievements. The public and media now take an unhealthy delight in toppling the famous from their perches and revealing them as all-too-fallible human-beings. Such treatment can apply to anyone in the public eye from princess to pop star and politician to actor. Once the idea of meeting someone famous used to cause a *frisson* of excitement, it is now more likely to provoke malicious gossip. Wearing dark glasses can be more of an invitation to ridicule and ruin than riches and repute.

The most vulnerable targets in today's ever-widening public eye are the royal family. The marriages or non-marriages of Prince Charles and the Princess of Wales and the Duke and Duchess of York have provoked more column inches than any other relationships in history. Initially admired for their glamorous, aristocratic lifestyles, the two couples gradually became news media targets, objects of fun and folly rather than figures of respect.

It has not always been so. Until the early 1980s, the royal family was a source of fascination to the British people, a group of figureheads who seemed to symbolize much that was fine and worthy about British life. The Queen was head of a growing British Commonwealth, an international ambassador able to represent Britain all over the world. She presided over such events as the state opening of parliament and trooping the colour and performed a ceremonial role when she and her family appeared in their finery at state occasions, public festivals, important openings and film previews. In a more material sense, the royals were a tourist attraction, able to add glitter and pageantry to the British way of life.

The first signs of change came in 1960 when the Queen and her advisers decided to hold a meeting to improve relations between the royal family and the news media. The meeting, which took place at the home of Lord Astor in Carlton House Terrace, was headed by the Queen and Prince Philip and attended by 500 editors, reporters and photographers from all the main media outlets in Britain and the Commonwealth. The Queen made a speech in which she asked the press to be more co-operative in their coverage of royal events. It was a peace offering to counter some bad press reports that had appeared in the previous few years. The *News of the World* correspondent said: 'The silent barrier across which royalty and the press usually regard each other warily as they go about their separate jobs, was crossed for the first time ... Some people have suggested that, if the essential mystique of royalty is to be retained, the press should not get to know them too well. We can confidently report, however, that as a result of the meeting, the palace and the press are currently on very good terms indeed.'

Relations between royalty and media remained warm and cordial. Then, in 1968, the Queen took the initiative again. This time she agreed to liaise with the BBC in a television documentary about the royal family. The film, which was made by the BBC producer Richard Cawston, showed a new, informal side to the royals. They could be seen eating together, playing with their corgis or just relaxing, a happy and domestic family enjoying a few simple, homely pleasures with plenty of good humour and laughter. The timing of the film – 30 June 1969 – was almost certainly calculated. The next day, Prince Charles was invested as Prince of Wales at Caernarfon Castle.

Then cracks started to appear. Far from giving the general public a discreet look at an ancient and revered institution, the press wanted more, and began to follow members of the royal family as they went about their official duties, taking photographs showing their moods and attitudes and recording their conversations and asides. Slowly the royals became public property, the groups of photographers turned into paparazzi who hunted in packs and the reporters became royal watchers, specially appointed by their newspapers to monitor the royal family's actions and behaviour. By the beginning of the 1980s, the Queen was already regretting her decision to be more open with the media. Her family had become more of a sideshow than a national institution.

The wedding of Prince Charles and the Princess of Wales in 1981 gave the public a different view of the royal family. Here was the heir to the throne marrying a beautiful young woman. It brought romance to the royals' relatively formal image. The Wales's public appearances and off-the-cuff remarks were featured in all the newspapers and television and radio stations. Royal watchers and fashion experts scrutinized the Princess's dress sense and hair styles and 'Princess Di' pictures were displayed on the front pages of the down-market and middle-market tabloids. Soon afterwards when Prince Andrew married the extrovert Sarah Ferguson, the reporters and paparazzi had another opportunity to dramatize the royal family. The tabloids talked about Shy Di and Fun-loving Fergie and journalists turned into amateur psychologists as they analysed the roles of the two princesses.

Soon the news media was taking more interest in the relationships of the two couples than in the royal family's daily activities. As a result, the British public's attitude changed from reverence to curiosity. There was also speculation about Prince Edward leaving the Royal Marines, Princess Margaret's relationship with Roddy Llewellyn, Princess Michael's father's wartime activities, Marina Ogilvy's baby, Prince Philip's occasional outspokenness and the state of the Princess Royal's marriage to Captain Mark Phillips. Throughout this restless and at times traumatic period, the Queen and Queen Mother maintained their dignity and reserve.

In an effort to preserve the royal image, the Queen recruited the radio broadcaster Dickie Arbiter from LBC in 1987 to handle the media's increasing preoccupation with the Wales's activities. Most of the time Arbiter found he was fending off sensational-style stories from the tabloids. In his book, *The New Royal Court*, Brian Hoey says: 'Nobody received more attention from the world's media than the Wales's. The Princess was the most photographed woman in the world and every newspaper and magazine from San Francisco to Singapore was willing to print the latest picture and the latest splash. Prince Charles, too, came in for more than his fair share of attention, but more often only when he spoke on controversial issues like the environment, modern architecture and the state of the English language.'

Arbiter spent half the week at Buckingham Palace and the other half at the Wales's home, St James's Palace, as he tried to cope with the burgeoning number of press inquiries. Arbiter's only blemish was when he told a reporter that the Princess Royal had referred to her brother Prince Andrew as 'an extremely yucky lung man'.

The Queen then gave Prince Charles a press adviser, Philip Mackie, a former newspaperman, to help out with overseas trips and special engagements. When Prince Charles's former equerry Major Hugh Lindsay was killed while skiing with the Prince at Klosters in Switzerland in 1988, it was Mackie who was called on to handle the delicate British and foreign news media coverage.

Soon afterwards Mackie was given a ten-point grilling by the *News of the World*. One of the questions he was asked was the Princess of Wales's hat size, which he said was a personal matter, another was the number of salmon Prince Charles had caught the previous year, a figure of which he said he had no idea. Finally, Mackie was asked whether it was the Prince or Princess who read the children their bedtime stories. Again he replied that he did not know. Mackie's answers were honest and discreet, reflecting the trivial nature of the inquiries put to him. If Mackie had been asked serious questions that he believed were in the public interest, he would have tried to answer them accordingly.

Soon after Mackie's appointment, the Queen increased her own team of press officers to three. From 1979 to 1987 her chief press secretary was Michael Shea. A former civil servant, Shea attracted some un-regal controversy when he indicated that the Queen did not like a number of Margaret Thatcher's policies. When he left his post to take up a similar position with Hanson Industries, he said: 'Those in the service of the royal family, or in some way involved with them, know what it is like to be hounded by the media ... my own harassment at my private home or when I was the centre of a story, are minor examples of what is an abhorrent daily occurrence.'

Not all royal press secretaries suffer media intrusion, however. Shea's successor, Robin Janvrin, former head of personnel at the Foreign and Commonwealth Office, spent a relatively controversy-free three years in the post before being promoted to assistant private secretary. The Queen then appointed her distant cousin Charles Anson, former head of press relations at merchant bankers Kleinwort Benson, to take over as press chief. Anson soon found himself the centre of unwanted attention when he referred to the Duchess of York as an unsuitable royal after her marriage break-up. He had committed the grave offence of taking sides among the royal family, provoking outrage from both media and establishment. Anson apologized for his remarks, pointing out the ambiguity of his role as a middle-man between several arguing royals. However, the news media showed their usual fickleness and the issue blew over within a few days. Anson also had to handle the tricky media coverage of the funding of repairs to Windsor Castle when it was damaged by fire, followed by the Queen's controversial decision to become a taxpayer.

Since the start of their marriage difficulties, the news media has given more coverage to the Wales's than any other well-known celebrities. The Princess Royal, sometimes criticized for her stand-offishness in the 1970s and 1980s, gets the occasional mention and photo-call for her work as president of the Save the Children Fund, the flame of Prince Edward's relationship with Sophie Rhys-Jones flickers from time to time, while the Duchess of York's spending habits are the subject of periodic tabloid scrutiny. But it is nothing as compared with the news media's obsession with the Wales's, and in 1993 the Queen gave Prince Charles his own press office at St James's Palace.

Today's royal PROs have to tread a delicate path between complete discretion to protect the royal family's interests and enough disclosure to satisfy the wiles of intrusive reporters. If they should ever so much as utter an indiscreet remark, they will be gloatingly pounced on by the popular tabloids. Probing questions on an indiscretion by the Duchess of York or the embarrassing revelations of a former member of the Buckingham Palace staff have to be answered as neutrally as possible. Otherwise the PRO will become as big a target as the royals he is trying to protect.

The prying of the news media has brought the role of the monarchy under increasing public scrutiny. A family once respected for its traditions and values became more human than its regal image once allowed it to be. When its relationships, money, attitudes and public behaviour were publicly debated, the remains of its mystique were removed; it turned into a tabloid caricature, a parody of its Spitting Image lookalikes. At present there is an uneasy truce between the royal family, the establishment and the news media. A growing core of republicans are arguing for change, while the conservationists are loath to alter a trusted formula. The future of the royal family may not be resolved for some time. Whatever happens, the media has ensured it will never be quite the same again.

However, there is no need for the royals to discard their dark glasses just yet, though the growing band of politicians forced to resign since 1992 might well have wished they had put theirs on a little sooner. The rewards of being in the public eye are often outweighed by the media pressures of having to be seen to be doing the right thing and setting a public example. Fame is rarely extinguished. Once a public figure, always a public figure.

Politics is Britain's most public profession. The nature of a politician's job and his accountability to the people means he is under constant news media scrutiny. One slip-up can unleash a deluge of exposure. Politics is also double-edged. Some politicians like to exploit their positions by getting their names into the newspapers and inviting themselves on to television and radio programmes. This makes them more vulnerable to media intrusion.

The House rule in politics is discretion. 'If many [MPs] reflect the flaws, foibles and interests of the rest of us, then they have a choice of making those known or of concealing them. Unfortunately in many areas they have no formal guidelines, other than common sense, prudence, caution and an eye to history, on how to behave,' says Alan Doig in *Westminster Babylon*.

The first big political scandal after the war was the Profumo Affair. The publicity shook Britain out of its nostalgic memories of two world war victories and its leadership of a growing commonwealth. It also gave Britain's European neighbours a hint of its susceptibility. They were amused to see a country famous for its ancient, democratic and avowedly high-principled style of government tainted by corruption. They could indulge in a little self-important mockery themselves. The news media revelations, which nearly brought down the government, also set the tone for a more intrusive style of political reporting. British MPs realized that, once defiled, they could not hide behind their positions of influence. They were accountable both for their public and private lives.

Former Liberal Party leader, Jeremy Thorpe's flair for publicity failed to protect him from months of rumour and supposition about his private life. When allegations of homosexuality and conspiracy to murder male model Norman Scott appeared, Thorpe opted not to make a full disclosure of what had occurred. So, led by the *Sunday Mirror*, the news media speculated about deals and cover-ups among leading members of the Liberal Party. Eventually, after a famous court case in 1978 when he was acquitted of all charges, Thorpe lost the support of the party he had worked so hard to establish, and resigned a broken man.

Neither Cecil Parkinson's reputation as an outstanding minister nor Mrs Thatcher's regard for his political skills could save him from the scandal of his affair and illegitimate daughter with Sara Keays. It was another case of a politician trying to preserve his public image until media coverage made it untenable. Ironically a *Times* profile before the scandal had said that the minister 'seems too good to be true; tall, handsome, charming and likeable ... the perfect constituency MP, intelligent without being intellectual, self-made, brilliantly supported by a politically committed wife – is there, one wonders, no flaw?'

Fame is no longer big news. The news media used to print pages of hagiography and hero-worship about favourite 1960s icons such as Twiggy, the Beatles and Brigitte Bardot. Today hero-worship is either short-lived or begrudging. Though she was in the spotlight for several years, admirers of the Princess of Wales were soon vying with her critics. Stars like Madonna, Cher and Tina Turner are idolized one day and demeaned the next with sensational allegations about their private lives, rumours of nip-and-tuck plastic surgery, torrid affairs or moments of foolish extravagance. The first international superstar to be discredited by the media was the former US president John F Kennedy. The tales of his two-timing and philandering were serialized in the *Sunday Times* and followed up by most of the other Fleet Street newspapers. Soon star after star from Marlon Brando and Frank Sinatra to Elizabeth Taylor and Tom Cruise were debunked by a cynical news media.

Journalist Raymond Snoddy says in *The Good, the Bad and the Unacceptable*: 'Enormous personal suffering can be caused by individual newspaper stories that are inaccurate or that intrude into people's privacy for no good reason. A few examples pass into the collective memory of the country, either because of the fame of those involved, the outrageousness of the behaviour alleged or the size of the libel damages eventually awarded. Such scandal stories damage the reputation of the press and perhaps play some part in coarsening the tone of public discourse.'

The publicity agent Max Clifford says: 'The British are hypocritical about gossip and scandals. They pretend to be shocked when they hear about wicked transgressions, but relish reading about them. Everyone, the world over, loves a good British scandal. The moral is: if you want to launch a scandal do it in London. The British newspaper proprietors know they sell newspapers, so they use their powers to make journalists pry into people's private lives, whether they like it or not. When a footballer like Paul Gascoigne breaks a leg, you get eight pages on his private life splashed across the tabloids, instead of a two-paragraph report about his medical condition.'

Sometimes the news media goes too far and creates its own noose. When the *Sun* leaped on spurious rumours that Elton John went to cocaine parties with rent-boys, the newspaper had taken the bait too quickly. It used only one original source for the allegations: a rent-boy. Several other rent-boys who later claimed they had been to parties with the pop star were discovered to be bank clerks used as part of an elaborate hoax played on the *Sun*. The newspaper's preposterous climax was that John was guarded by rottweilers – 'silent assassins' whose voice-boxes had been surgically removed – when in fact he owned several healthy alsatians. The publication of these fabricated stories resulted in a successful £1 million libel action against the newspaper.

Media speculation is one of modern journalism's favourite ploys. Mischievous journalists use this largely artificial device to spice up their stories about the famous, sometimes stretching it so far that it turns into fantasy. The problem is that not all public personalities are as adept or well-represented as Elton John. When a story emerges carrying pages of unwarranted conjecture its subject may not know how to handle it, choosing to ignore it, in which case the publicity may carry on regardless. Alternatively he or she may deny it, but not take legal action, which could provoke more speculation.

It is often the most popular media personalities that suffer the nastiest slurs. When an *Observer* story implied that Conservative MP Edwina Currie was ruthless and uncaring, she successfully sued the newspaper. However, the only reason the newspaper printed the story in the first place was because she was a popular public figure. If she had been an inconspicuous Conservative back-bencher, they would not have bothered.

People who do good and worthy work often suffer the most media abuse, particularly if they are famous. The television presenter and founder of the charity Childline, Esther Rantzen, successfully sued the *People* when they impugned her integrity over the case of a child abuser. She told the High Court: 'In my profession, one becomes very accustomed to being criticized. Frankly, if I don't like people saying I am too old, too ugly or the wrong person to do my job then I must lead a more sheltered life. But this struck at the heart of what I believe to be the most important thing that I am employed to do, that aspect of my work that protects children.'

Actors and actresses make glamorous media targets. Tabloids endlessly expose the indiscretions of soap stars they know their readers are familiar with. Yet, like the Freddie Starr

Ate My Hamster story, they are often just good publicity stunts to boost the actor's career. When Liz Hurley, who had previously acted in only one film, appeared at a major première in a dress held together with safety pins, her career soared overnight. She was asked to make commercials for Estée Lauder, the cosmetics manufacturer, switched on the Christmas lights in Oxford Street, and received several film offers. Sometimes the coverage is more callous. When it was announced that the actor Nigel Hawthorne had been nominated for an Oscar, the Fleet Street tabloids used it as an excuse to reveal that he was gay.

Pop stars and sportsmen actively woo the press to boost their careers. A few mentions in the tabloid pop columns or plugs on the airwaves can help an up-and-coming singer gain valuable record, video and CD contracts. Media coverage also keeps sportsmen in the public eye and helps them win lucrative sponsorships. However the lure of money brings temptation as well as reward. High transfer fees and sponsorships have made football particularly vulnerable. Several managers, agents and football stars have been accused in the media of receiving bungs during transfer deals, of match-fixing and of violence.

Decrying the famous sells more newspapers than deifying them. Many able and ambitious people are reluctant to take up public positions in politics, commerce and the arts because of the risk of media intrusion into their private lives. It is a hypocritical dilemma. For it is doubtful whether the private lives of several national newspaper editors would stand up to scrutiny. We are reaching a stage where public figures will have to wear dark glasses when walking down the street more for fear of public recrimination than recognition. The news media seems to enjoy taking away their freedom and hard-won prestige. Envy is not the main cause, though many aspiring journalists covet fame. Fashion is the real culprit. In an age of reason and intellect-worship, it is more rewarding to demean public figures than to praise them. It is more newsworthy, too.

7

The Tory Story

'Politics is show-business for ugly people.'

Dermot Purgavie, foreign correspondent

Newspapers, radio and television are modern versions of the messengers of ancient Greece. Just as the famous runners, Euchidas and Pheidippides, carried the news of battles with the Persians back to the Greek emperor and his court, so too does the news media relay the highlights of the day's events and mishaps to the British general public. It is arguable whether it does so as effectively. The media's simplicity of description is often coloured by political, subjective and editorial bias and a need to entertain its audience. But the basic principle of passing on knowledge to which only it has been privy is the same. It is the relaying of the news that has changed over the centuries. Today's reports are studied by a number of editors and sub-editors and must go through complex computer networks and recording systems before reaching the public. As a result, by the time it is published the news has often lost its spontaneity. Instead of being the true *vox populi*, like the Greek messengers and the scribes in the Roman market-place, today's

reporters are media middle-men paid to boost their newspapers' readership. But modern journalism has not always been
so.

When *The Times* – or *Universal Daily Register* as it was then
known – was first published in 1785, its aim was to reflect the
changing moods of public opinion and thought and to report
on the activities of the government; no more no less. It was a
four-page information sheet with a few well-chosen advertisements which 'in its politics, will be of no party' according to
its editor and printer, John Walter.

Then Thomas Barnes, who became editor of *The Times* in
1817, brought a political element into the newspaper,
announcing that he liked to 'put a little devil' into stories.
Initially he supported the Whig administration of Lord Grey. In
1834, he switched to the Conservatives and according to one
observer 'gave a most remarkable demonstration of the power
of the instrument he had partly created'. *The Times*'s
circulation was 30,000 higher than any other national
newspaper, and Barnes began to dictate terms to the
Conservative party, both privately and in his daily columns. It
was the first time a British newspaper had publicly sided with a
political party.

In the mid-nineteenth century, newspapers tended to ally
with one party or the other – the Whigs or the Tories. It was a
fickle policy. After supporting the government for a few
months, the day's newspapers would suddenly move over to the
opposition and carry on doing so until they changed their
minds again. *The Times* was taken particularly seriously by
Victorian politicians. The Whig reformer William Cobden
refused to take it into his home because of its opinions, while in
1853 the foreign secretary, William Clarendon, said: 'As its
circulation is enormous and its influence abroad is very great, a
government must take its support on the terms it chooses to put
it.' *The Times* soon earned a reputation as The Thunderer.

At the start of the twentieth century, the national press's
political loyalties were evenly divided. The *Daily News* and the
Daily Chronicle were affiliated, both financially and politically,

to the Liberal party; the *Observer, Globe, Standard* and *Pall Mall Gazette* received secret funds from the Unionist party and paid them back in column inches; while a Conservative syndicate headed by the Duke of Northumberland bought and ran the *Morning Post*.

The first major media proprietors to actively support the Conservatives were Lords Northcliffe, Rothermere and Beaverbrook. Between 1919 and 1922, Rothermere and Northcliffe mounted a fierce campaign against Lloyd George's coalition government with editorials in *The Times, Daily Mail, Daily Mirror*, and the London *Evening News*. Their propaganda was so effective that it helped to abolish the post-war Shipping, Munitions and Food Ministries and persuaded several private companies to buy state-owned factories and shipyards. Aided by Lord Beaverbrook, owner of the *Daily* and *Sunday Express*, their support for the Conservatives helped the party win the 1922 general election.

When the three proprietors decided to back the smaller, more obscure Empire Party, Conservative leader Stanley Baldwin ran an aggressive public campaign against them, using leaflet drives, public speeches, columns in rival newspapers and House of Commons proclamations, to discredit the Fleet Street barons. The campaign succeeded. Worried by its effects on the sales and profits of their newspapers, the barons made their peace with the Conservatives and pledged to support them again.

After the Second World War, most national newspapers were apolitical. Historian Stephen Koss is quoted in *Power Without Responsibility*: 'Newspapers grew steadily more catholic and less partisan in their ordinary news coverage. When confronted by a general election, they generally expressed a party preference, but always with at least a gesture of pragmatism and often for a different party from the one they had previously endorsed.' There were no dominant press barons to bemuse the public during the 1950s and 1960s. The major post-war proprietor was the Canadian Lord Thomson who bought the Kemsley empire of regional newspapers in 1959 and *The Times* and *Sunday Times* in 1967. Thomson was not an interventionist, preferring to leave his newspapers' politics to his editors.

Signs of a trend to Toryism occurred in 1969 when Rupert Murdoch began his takeover of British newspapers. Murdoch, a self-confessed socialist at Oxford University, became increasingly right wing as his empire expanded. During the 1974 general election, the *Sun* switched its allegiance from Labour to Conservative, even though most of its readers were left-wing trade-unionists and Labour Party supporters. Murdoch changed the paper into a tabloid, made it more sensational, and employed the tough no-nonsense Yorkshireman, Larry Lamb, to run it. When Kelvin MacKenzie joined as editor in 1981, the paper became both xenophobic and Thatcherite. Its readers were told to despise the French in headlines such as 'Up Yours, Delors' and 'Hop Off You Frogs', vilify the Argentinians during the Falklands War with slogans like 'We'll Smash 'Em', and slammed the Labour Party during elections with banners like 'Labour Picks Rent-Boy As School Boss', 'Labour Uses Gay Jimi To Win Over Young Voters' and 'Superstar Maggie Is A Wow At Wembley'. The *News of the World* also stayed firmly to the right after Murdoch bought the paper in 1969, one editor, Barry Askew, staying in his post for only nine months because of his left-wing views. During the 1980s, *The Times* and *Sunday Times* also became Murdoch-Thatcherites.

Recently Murdoch's national newspapers have shown a muted sympathy for the Labour Party. However, in the 1970s and 1980s, Murdoch often visited the editorial offices of his papers, chatting with the executives and checking the tone of the main stories. If he saw a leader that was insufficiently Thatcherite, he would sit down at a computer screen and rewrite it himself. The only newspaper that escaped the Australian tycoon's scrutiny was *Today* which made a determined effort to stay left of centre, supporting environmental issues and backing the Green Party.

Victor Matthews, whose Trafalgar House group bought the *Daily* and *Sunday Express* and *Daily Star* in 1977, steered the papers even further right than they had traditionally stood. When Matthews resigned as the Express group's proprietor in 1985, he was made a life peer by Margaret Thatcher for his papers' support for the Conservative party. Lord Stevens, who took over from Lord Matthews, maintained the Tory tradition, telling a rival newspaper: 'I would not be happy to be associated with a left-wing paper. I suppose the papers echo my political views – I do interfere and say enough is enough.'

The *Daily Telegraph* is a little like a Tory grandee. Known as the Daily Torygraph, it is reliable, consistent and, until recently, unflinchingly loyal to the Conservative Party. Its Tory allegiance began soon after the newspaper's founding in 1855, and there have been times since then when its affinity has been so strong that it has preferred to follow the party line than take any initiatives of its own. When the Canadian Conrad Black took over the *Daily* and *Sunday Telegraph* he proved a devoted Thatcherite, telling Margaret Thatcher's last Conservative Party conference that his newspapers' aim was to 'safeguard the constitution of this sovereign nation'. Though a stout defender of upper-middle-class values, the *Daily Telegraph* became more radical under Max Hastings's editorship, sometimes criticizing government policies and condemning ministers for rash decisions.

Lord Rothermere leaves most of the day-to-day running of the *Daily Mail* to the chairman of Associated Newspapers, Sir David English. Both have modelled the *Daily Mail* on the staunch beliefs and attitudes of the Conservative middle classes. The paper supports traditional values and the family unit, extols safe, high-street fashions and the role of career women and rarely criticizes the government. Its two stablemates, the *Mail on Sunday* and the London *Evening Standard*, follow a similar policy.

When the *People* was launched in 1881, it won instant approval from the Unionist Party (the party later amalgamated with the Conservatives) who said 'it will go far to break down the almost complete monopoly of the popular Sunday Press, at present enjoyed by the Radical Party'. It remained a

Conservative newspaper until it was bought by the Mirror Group, since when it has been unashamedly down-market and, like its *Daily Mirror* stablemate, more left than right wing.

The *Daily Mirror* was founded in 1903 by Lord Northcliffe as a women's picture tabloid. Guy Bartholomew, the newspaper's editorial director from 1934 to 1951, made it a paper of the masses, with bright, snappy stories, big pictures and bold headlines. Hugh Cudlipp, Bartholomew's successor, turned the *Daily Mirror* into a sharp, campaigning newspaper of the left. To increase its circulation, the newspaper also pledged itself to the Labour Party. The new *Mirror* was so popular that, on Coronation Day 1953, it sold seven million copies, a figure never equalled by a national newspaper before or since. Recently the newspaper continued its support for the Labour Party, though there have been signs of a more muted political approach by Mirror Group Newspapers' new board of directors headed by David Montgomery. The *Sunday Mirror* was launched in 1915 as the *Sunday Pictorial*. It has never had a particularly strong political content. Retitled the *Sunday Mirror* in 1963, it has remained a pinkish version of the *Daily Mirror*.

The *Guardian*, which first appeared as the *Manchester Guardian* in 1821, was edited from 1872 until 1929 by C P Scott, when it earned a reputation as the 'supreme expression of the liberal spirit'. It has been a liberal, free-thinking newspaper under Alastair Hetherington from 1956 to 1975, Peter Preston from 1975 to 1995 and Alan Rusbridger since then. The *Observer*, which is now owned by the Guardian Trust, is Britain's oldest Sunday newspaper. Founded in 1791, its aims were lofty and high-principled. During the mid-nineteenth century, Lord Palmerston, the Whig foreign secretary, wrote *Observer* leaders supporting his own policies and also paying the newspaper from secret service funds. Its most famous editor was J L Garvin who saved it from the Fleet Street gutter into which he said it was falling in 1905 and boosted its circulation to more than 200,000 by the time he retired in 1942. The *Observer* has continued to be a radical left-wing newspaper, its two principal post-war editors being David Astor (1948–1975) and Donald Trelford (1975–1993).

The *Independent* and *Independent on Sunday* have remained moderate, centrist newspapers since they were founded. The *Independent* was an enthusiastic supporter of the SDP until the party's demise in 1989. Since then, both newspapers have tried to give well-reasoned and dispassionate views on the political activities of the day.

Perhaps the most fascinating chapter in the modern Tory story is the emergence of the Ingham Effect. Bernard Ingham, who was Mrs Thatcher's chief press secretary for 11 years, helped to project his leader and her staunch political views with single-minded passion. Ingham trained as a reporter on the *Hebden Bridge Times* before joining the *Yorkshire Post* and becoming a *Guardian* labour correspondent. He moved into public relations as a press officer to the Prices and Incomes Board and had two spells as head of information at the departments of employment and energy, where he was also an under-secretary in the energy conservation division.

He became Mrs Thatcher's press chief in 1979. Though he had never known or worked with her before, Ingham was soon being referred to as Thatcher's ventriloquist. One observer said of the closeness of their alliance: 'It's as if you are talking to the prime minister herself. Even the emphasis is rarely wrong. You would take him for a right-wing monetarist.' Each day, Ingham held briefings with lobby correspondents at Number 10 when he dutifully echoed his leader's political line. If a journalist did not publish what Ingham wanted, he would cajole him at the next day's briefing.

Ingham was an arch-manipulator. Many of his briefings resembled episodes from the BBC television series *Yes, Minister* for all the clichés, evasive answers and government jargon he managed to employ. Like all good PROs, Ingham was an expert at suppressing important information and using red herrings to put journalists off the scent of a good story. It was a role he performed so cleverly that many newspapers, television and radio programmes became unwitting spokesmen for the Conservative Party.

Ingham also used the 'leak' to its best advantage. He would tell journalists, in confidence, about supposed prime ministerial secrets and events that were about to happen – all under the banner of Exclusives – when most of the time, both the government and prime minister were intending to print these 'secrets' anyway.

Ingham helped sell Mrs Thatcher and her brand of Toryism throughout three terms in office. He and Mrs Thatcher's advisers helped preen her image, improved her microphone techniques, modulated her rather shrill speaking voice, changed her hair style, and introduced a Sincerity Machine for televised speeches projecting the contents of her speech on to two hidden lecterns, which enabled her to move her head from side to side in apparent deference to her audience.

Thatcher was touted to the right-wing Fleet Street newspapers and the less Conservative radio and television stations as a 'conviction politician'. Sometimes, if her matriarchal image was threatened by a dissenting colleague, it fell to Ingham to discredit him at his daily briefings with journalists. One victim, John Biffen, who was sacked from his post as leader of the House of Commons, has said that Ingham was 'only an instrument of the prime ministerial will, the sewer and not the sewage.'

Mrs Thatcher was the ideal media personality. Strong and dictatorial, she provided the Tory press, and indirectly their readers, with the figurehead the country seemed to need. They could see her as Boadicea leading her subjects out of political turmoil. Such was her conviction that she would refer to the country as Thatcher's Britain and her voters as Thatcher's Children during media interviews. Thatcher heroine-worship reached its peak during the Falklands War, especially in the down-market and middle-market tabloids who made her conquests sound like Second World War victories. Elections became Tory media propaganda campaigns, polls were used by the right-wing newspapers to massage electoral opinion, while television profiles enhanced the Tory's new doctrine of Victorian values. In the two months before the 1983 general election, Mrs Thatcher gave 16 full-length television interviews on the four major networks.

The most effective of Mrs Thatcher's three pre-election media campaigns was in 1987. The pro-Tory *Daily Mail* and *Sun* vied to see which newspaper could produce the most 'loony left' stories. The zaniest was printed by the *Sun* which said Labour's Bernie Grant, leader of Haringey Council, had told his employees that they could only drink coffee from left-wing Nicaragua. Its headline was: 'Barmy Bernie is going Coffee-Potty – staff must drink Marxist brew'. The *Sun* also said that Labour-controlled Brent Council had replaced its black bin-liners with green ones for racial reasons. Then both papers ran stories that Labour's Hackney Council had declared the word 'manhole' sexist and banned the nursery rhyme 'Baa Baa Black Sheep' on racist grounds. The *Sun* eventually won the 'loony left' contest, with eleven stories to the *Daily Mail*'s seven.

Most of Britain's national newspapers became Mrs Thatcher's political champions. Four editors were knighted – Sir Larry Lamb (*Sun*), Sir David English (*Daily Mail*), Sir Nicholas Lloyd (*Daily Express*) and Sir John Junor (*Sunday Express*) – for their services to the Conservative Party; and Mrs Thatcher and Bernard Ingham spent her last term of office exploiting the news media at every possible opportunity. The only note of dissension was saved for the BBC when Mrs Thatcher pointed out in a widely publicized statement that the corporation had run more pro-Labour than pro-Tory interviews before general elections and had held too many late-night, left-wing discussion programmes. The BBC loftily pointed out that they had done their best to be objective in their political coverage.

Mrs Thatcher and the Ingham Effect was the most blatant example of news-media management this century. In his book, *Treacherous Estate*, journalist Michael Leapman says: 'There is nothing undemocratic about a government seeking to ensure exposure for its views or favourable publicity for its actions, so long as the papers are free to reject its pressures if they so wish.

It is more worrying when governments, not content merely with trying to exert influence, seek the means to enforce control over what goes into the press. Mrs Thatcher and her administration gave a number of signs of coveting such powers.'

John Major is a very different type of media operator from Margaret Thatcher. Unlike his predecessor, he has no underlying strategy in his dealings with newspapers and television. He also lacks her vote-winning charisma. So, in the months before the 1992 election, the news media turned to the opinion polls to do their Tory electioneering for them, exploiting the polls mercilessly until they began to hint at a Labour victory. Then, three days before the election, Labour's shadow chancellor John Smith announced that his party would raise taxation if elected. It was a guaranteed vote-loser and a gift to the Tory press. The Conservatives virtually won the election by default. Perhaps the wittiest piece of propaganda appeared on the eve of the election when the *Sun* published a picture of Labour leader Neil Kinnock with a light bulb over his head. Underneath, it ran the caption: 'If Neil Kinnock wins today, will the last person to leave Britain please turn the lights out.' John Major's frequent appearances on a soap box also helped his claim to lead the country as Public Orator Number One.

All modern governments exploit the news media to help them stay in power, whether by democratic means or foul. One of the most unpleasant techniques is the dirty tricks campaign. The idea is to print a number of unsavoury facts about a person or group of people so as to publicly undermine them. Conservative Central Office attempted to upset the Liberal Democrats' campaign during the run-up to the 1992 election by sending a dossier about their leader Paddy Ashdown to the BBC's *Newsnight* programme. However the BBC did not use it. A similar ploy was used by his opponents against John Redwood during the 1995 Conservative leadership contest with John Major.

Not all propaganda techniques are so aggressive however. One of the most successful is the lobby system, started in 1885 by the Whig prime minister William Gladstone to boost his administration's relations with the press. Not unlike the Number Ten briefing, a select band of journalists is given regular briefings by politicians and press spokesmen wishing to sell on favourite policies and issues outside parliamentary business time at the House of Commons. Journalists in the lobby are not allowed to reveal it as their source of information, which merely adds to their stories' exclusive off-the-record flavour and protects the politicians and spokesmen involved from any repercussions.

The idea of leaking government information to the press also began in the late nineteenth century when a spate of leaks from the civil service prompted premier Gladstone to send out a memo saying: 'Such breaches of official confidence are of the gravest character which a public officer can commit.' Today, however, the parliamentary leak is looked on as a valuable source of propaganda. The most common is the official leak, which is a piece of government, civil service or party information that a press officer has been authorized to pass on to the media. There is also the unofficial leak, which, because of its clandestine nature, is a more speculative item of news with some risk attached. When a press officer is passing on an unofficial leak, he usually does it to a specially selected journalist. Naturally unauthorized leaks seep into the system from time to time, the culprits often ending up in court. During one particularly leaky period in Margaret Thatcher's administration, Bernard Ingham sent a memo to the civil service pointing out: 'Moles who do not own up risk being reclassified as rats.'

Leaks make journalists believe they have been given a strong story, as well as helping the government sell propaganda. Sometimes the government uses a leak to pass on a piece of disinformation – information used to deflect the public from the truth: a leaked story about fewer people on hospital waiting lists could be a cover-up for a recent rise in the number of people waiting to get on the lists in the first place.

To be on the safe side, each department of state has spokespersons specially briefed to talk to the news media. They are supported by the Central Office of Information which, like a government PR agency, puts the daily press announcements of the government and civil service into clear, well-presented leaflets, brochures and booklets. The COI has its own team of producers who make films and hold radio talks on different aspects of departmental work. It also has a department that handles exhibitions and conferences on government affairs.

Ministry PROs and the COI are meant to act as a barrier against politicians' indiscretions and excesses. However Sir Ian Gilmour, the former Conservative cabinet minister, sees it differently: 'The real secrecy of British government is partly camouflaged by the mass of information and statistics fed out by government departments and by the activities of government public relations officers.'

As we all know, politicians exploit the media to boost their careers. Photo-opportunities and pre-planned interviews are tools of the modern politician's trade. At any given opportunity, a Minister or MP will telephone a producer or editor to let him air his views about the latest government decision or opposition *faux pas*. The ideal moments for media exposure are major policy announcements, elections and resignations. Some MPs, such as Ken Livingstone, Edwina Currie, David Mellor and Jerry Hayes also make entertaining quiz and chat-show guests.

Many politicians attend courses on how to handle the media. The standard technique seems to be: if asked a question you don't wish to answer, use an evasive reply, change the subject or use the opportunity to promote a new aspect of party policy. Otherwise ignore the question altogether and continue where you had previously left off. Another popular technique is to interrupt the questioner in mid-flow as often as possible. Both Neil Kinnock and Margaret Thatcher, followed by John Major and Tony Blair, were taught their craft by specially commissioned media specialists, sometimes spending two or three hours at one sitting rehearsing their new-found techniques. Such training helps them cope with skilful interviewers whose questions are often devised to catch them out and expose the apparent sham of their policies and decisions. Margaret Thatcher used to turn interviews to her advantage by lecturing her questioners on what questions they should ask her and pointing out how they should conduct the interview.

Even if you studiously try to avoid them, it is sometimes impossible to escape weekly programmes and feature articles about politicians, parties and parliament. Politics takes up more space and air-time than any other subject in the British news media and has given members of the press an all-pervasive role as commentators on British life. The media is free to praise or condemn government decisions, interrogate Ministers and MPs, make political judgements and recommend policies it supports – not unlike the role of Her Majesty's Opposition. Modern governments invariably find it is the news media, not the opposition parties, they have to answer to when running the country.

8

Media Wars

'In wartime, truth is so precious that she should always be attended by a bodyguard of lies.'

Sir Winston Churchill

We live in a restless society in which wars, violence and conflict have far greater media appeal than peace and harmony. Man's inhumanity to man rather than his acts of goodness make the headlines. An attack on a neighbour by crowbar-wielding thugs creates a bigger stir in the local community than a tree surgeon being presented with a conservation award, while a story about an air attack in Angola will attract more news media coverage than one about a peace pact in the Arabian Gulf. Peace fails to arouse the senses; it lacks war's brio and excitement, and whatever the merits of their causes, conscientious objectors receive little sympathy from the general public or the news media. Journalists, like politicians and servicemen, are life's natural combatants. Wars and conflicts give them the opportunity to play power games with their readers, display bravery at the front and revive patriotic memories of two world wars.

100

Before Vietnam, war coverage was confined to newspapers and the radio. Television was in its infancy and did not have the manpower or resources to devote to coverage of troublespots. The Vietnam War attracted millions of column inches and graphic black-and-white pictures in the newspapers for 21 years, while television showed isolated incidents and ran occasional documentaries about the war's futility, and the measured tones of BBC radio newsreaders gave details of the latest attacks and troop movements. The Vietnam War became the event without an ending.

The 1982 Falklands War was the first conflict to attract significant television coverage in Britain. Live reports and animated discussions about strategy and tactics accompanied frequent news flashes and gung-ho victories. Realizing the war's media potential, the Conservative government cunningly exploited it to try to restore their fortunes with the electorate. Soon after prime minister Margaret Thatcher heard the Argentinians were about to invade the Falkland Islands, she called a meeting of her senior cabinet ministers, pointing out the seriousness of the assault and its value as a media opportunity. Mrs Thatcher's popularity had been waning among the British electorate and she knew her political survival depended on how she handled any future hostilities with the Argentinians. So, as soon as they invaded, Mrs Thatcher and her chief press officer Bernard Ingham mounted a calculated pre-election publicity campaign to win support for the Conservative government.

At first, the Royal Navy barred all press representatives from travelling with the British Task Force. Then Ingham intervened and they agreed to take five newspaper reporters plus two television reporters and a three-man camera crew. This caused uproar among the major news media, who accused the Royal Navy of favouritism. Ingham intervened again and the Navy agreed to allow 29 pressmen to travel on the outgoing ships. Then Thatcher seized her opportunity. She told the mainly pro-Tory press corps that she wanted them to report the ensuing conflict as a 'Good News War'.

When they reached the islands, correspondents and reporters found they were being closely chaperoned by Ministry of Defence and Royal Navy PROs. Outgoing reports were scrutinized by the military communications network, while television films had to be played and edited for several days by the authorities before being sent back to Britain. BBC and ITN executives were furious, arguing that they could have transmitted their films directly to Britain via satellite from HMS *Hermes*, an aircraft carrier anchored near the southern tip of the Falklands. But Mrs Thatcher's government officials retorted that pictures of the dead and dying would upset British morale. Meanwhile, Army and Navy intelligence censored any stories they believed might damage the British cause, pushing those they did not consider one-sided enough to the back of the transmission queue. It meant many important war stories missed their deadlines.

Back in Britain, the main defence correspondents were given on-the-record briefings by the Ministry of Defence's acting PRO, Ian Macdonald. This did not satisfy Ingham. He changed these to 'off-the-record' briefings – similar to those given to parliamentary lobby correspondents – to give them a more exclusive tone, though Macdonald explained rather weakly that the change was to 'keep the media sweet and on our side'. One of the correspondents, the BBC's political editor John Cole said: 'More effort than usual was being made to feed the media the "right" information.' And the right information meant any propaganda that kept the Conservatives ahead in the British opinion polls. As the Falklands War historian, David Held, says: 'Through the use of D-notices and a whole package of rules, conventions and laws pertaining to secrecy ... the government was able to keep a remarkable amount of information to itself, offering only a highly selective impression, and making it very hard to discern exactly what was happening and in whose interest.'

Some of the most obvious examples of Conservative propaganda appeared on nightly television programmes, as military experts speculated about British and Argentinian tactics and manoeuvres with the main war pundits, David Dimbleby, Peter Snow and Robin Day. Soon their inside knowledge and apparent grasp of British policy earned them the sobriquet the 'Armchair Generals'. Unfortunately, even they were used in the propaganda stakes, at one point announcing that British troops had decided not to invade the main Argentinian port of San Carlos. Two days later the British invaded.

Not all Fleet Street newspapers favoured war. Some believed the dispute over the Islands' sovereignty could be solved by negotiation, not bloodshed and the loss of young lives. However these misgivings were countered by rousing House of Commons speeches from leading Conservatives who called for British glory in the face of adversity.

In Fleet Street, the news desks of the pro-Tory newspapers resembled war rooms, as news editors and reporters treated Falklands War coverage like a military operation. The *Sun*, as usual, went further than all the others, setting up its own war desk. Ever the shrewd newsman Kelvin MacKenzie had heard rumours of an Argentinian invasion weeks before and already had a reporter posted on the Islands when the war began. News editor Tom Petrie was the *Sun*'s commander and wore a khaki cap; all women reporters were referred to as Wrens, the prettiest, Muriel Burden, being voted 'Darling of the Fleet'; and any reporter who brought in a good story was promoted to 'colonel'. A picture of Winston Churchill hovered over Petrie's head next to a large map of the Falkland Islands bedecked with small coloured flags to show the changing positions of the British and Argentinian ships. Master of operations was General MacKenzie, who issued commands with the flick of a general's baton.

Each day the *Sun* carried the slogan 'The Paper That Supports Our Boys' under its masthead, and handed out 'The *Sun* Says Good Luck Lads' leaflets to its readers. The newspaper's patriotic fervour was reflected in its headlines, from 'We'll Smash 'Em', to 'The *Sun* Says Knickers to the Argentinians' and finally the controversial 'Gotcha' when the Argentine ship, the *General Belgrano*, was sunk by a British torpedo. Soon it was using the word Flak-lands instead of Falklands in its stories. The Conservatives lapped it up. It was all part of the fighting spirit they were trying to impart to the British electorate.

Back in Westminster, Ingham's and Thatcher's news massaging went on behind the scenes. Cover-ups were one of their favourite ploys. When, unknown to the British media, two helicopters crashed and several soldiers were killed during the operation to take the Falklands town of South Georgia, Mrs Thatcher arranged a pre-planned news conference outside Number 10 Downing Street with defence secretary John Nott, announcing to the assembled news media that it had been a stirring British victory with no casualties. Not all the reporters were taken in, however. Several times Thatcher was asked probing questions which she refused to answer and, turning on her heel, told the newsmen to 'rejoice' in a famous British triumph.

Next day, the pro-Tory *Daily Telegraph*, described the British troops as 'Cockleshell Heroes' on its front page, while a more sceptical Max Hastings, then working for the London *Evening Standard*, said: 'The reports published in the London newspapers of the way in which South Georgia was taken were complete rubbish from beginning to end.'

Then the Conservative hype began to jar. Several disenchanted reporters saw cracks in the patriotic approach of the Army, Navy and Defence press officers and referred to it as the 'Tory War'. This view was further compounded when Task Force commander, Admiral Sandy Woodward, used a sporting metaphor to describe the final assault on the Islands: 'This is the run-up to the big match which in my view should be a walk-over. We were told the Argentinians would be a tough lot, but they were quick to throw in the towel.'

When, a few days later, the BBC's Peter Snow hinted on air that there might be bias in the British news coverage, a furious Mrs Thatcher called a meeting between 100 Conservative MPs and the BBC's two senior executives, chairman George Howard and director-general-designate Alasdair Milne. Several MPs asked for the BBC executives' resignation. However, an unusually mellow Mrs Thatcher opted for a severe rebuke instead. Later the managing director of BBC Radio, Richard Francis, commented: 'Our job is not jingo. It is to provide the most reliable account of confusing and worrying events. Truth is the best propaganda.'

But perhaps the most famous piece of Falklands propaganda was the sinking of the *Belgrano*. Led by the *Sun*'s 'Gotcha', the incident in which 386 people died was given jubilant coverage by the popular tabloids and almost equally excitable acclaim by the middle-market ones. At the time Mrs Thatcher insisted the ship was sailing towards the British Task Force and therefore posed an obvious threat, which led to much media speculation and a severe television grilling by a sceptical David Frost. It was an unauthorized leak by the civil servant Clive Ponting two years later that revealed the real truth of the issue – that the *Belgrano* was in fact sailing away from the Task Force and was outside territorial waters when it was sunk.

Three weeks later, British troops conquered the key beach-head of Port San Carlos. To 'celebrate' victory, John Nott asked the news media to print a photograph of a British soldier drinking tea with a thankful-looking islander. Two weeks before, the controversial award-winning photographer Don McCullin, of the *Sunday Times*, had been refused permission to go to the Islands in case his pictures told a more raw and revealing story.

In the end Mrs Thatcher's opportunism became even too much for the Task Force. Just before Goose Green, the War's last major conflict, she told BBC Radio's World Service programme that British troops were about to invade the town – against the advice of the commanders who wished to keep it confidential in case the Argentinians should find out. Then during the invasion, in her quest for personal glory, she announced a British victory, although hostilities were still going on. Mrs Thatcher's actions provoked an irate response from Colonel H Jones, commander of the Second Parachute Battalion, who threatened to sue Mrs Thatcher and John Nott if any lives were lost during the battle.

After the invasion, the British local elections produced a last-minute swing to the Conservatives. The Falklands War had won them the day, and Mrs Thatcher and her ministers continued to bask in the glory of 'her' victory until the general election the following year when the Conservatives won by a larger-than-expected majority.

The Falklands was a war of disinformation and double-take. It was also a cautionary tale to the news media of how a government could manipulate coverage for its own political gain. It is unlikely that the media will allow any future government to get away with such blatant opportunism.

The 1991 Gulf War was more of an international affair and had far less media appeal for the British government. To the average television viewer it seemed more like a giant firework display than a serious conflict. Each night viewers tuned in and watched as flurries of Iraqi Scuds lit up the sky and cascaded down on their targets like shooting stars, broken by the occasional ball-of-fire as one of them was hit by an Israeli Patriot. Programmes about the war were regularly shown on BBC and ITV, while Channel 4 gave viewers a 24-hour display via CNN, the American television network. Fleet Street treated the Gulf War as a pre-eminently American conflict rather than an exclusively British one. It did not have the hype value of the Falklands War.

In a style reminiscent of the Falklands, the foreign press corps was tightly cordoned by US military PROs, who used the war as an American propaganda exercise, with CNN as its main media outlet. The main foreign correspondents were divided into press pools and ferried daily to selected troublespots and hospital casualty units by US Army jeeps where they were given heavily censored briefings about the war's progress. The PROs were soon being referred to as the Pentagon parrots by a somewhat jaded press corps who were anxious to see some real action. Another group of correspondents based at a hotel near Riyadh airport in Saudi Arabia were only allowed to send their reports from a little booth next to the hotel's turquoise-tinted swimming pool.

The writer Bruce Cumings says in his book, *War and Television*: 'The Pentagon's anal retentive press handlers massaged the five per cent of the 1,000-odd journalists in Saudi Arabia lucky enough to get admitted to the Riyadh press pool, while smaller pools herded everyone else around. The Pentagon photographed, fingerprinted and gave detailed marching orders to the reporters; it required all stories to be submitted for "security review"; no one could report details of operations, numbers of troops, or specific locations; no journalists could report from front-line units, tank or artillery units, or from helicopters or other aircraft, except in small press pools.'

A few journalists, included Robert Fisk of the *Independent*, Martin Woollacott of the *Guardian*, and the BBC's John Simpson, managed to avoid the press pools and get into the thick of the action. Simpson, who spent six months in Bagdhad before being expelled by the Iraqis, says: 'The biggest dilemma I faced was whether to tell the truth and face being thrown out, or hold back the salient facts and please everybody at the same time. The problem is that no war can be covered objectively if your country is taking part, and one of the disadvantages of reporting the Gulf War for the BBC was that, apart from having to avoid the Ministry of Defence's propaganda, I had to bear in mind that the average member of the public was not interested in hearing about the activities of the enemy.'

In Britain, the Armchair Generals spoke about the war's strategies on television, referring to it as the Gaffe War when it was discovered that 70 per cent of the bombs dropped by the Americans missed their targets and that many Israeli Scuds hit friendly bases instead of enemy ones. Sometimes the British television and newspaper coverage resembled Hollywood melodrama, featuring the American General 'Storming' Norman Schwarzkopf leading his troops into battle across the desert sands. In time, CNN's coverage affected the morale of the Iraqi people. Whenever there was an American or Allied attack, they panicked and ran out into the open in a desperate search for cover, thus causing a dramatic rise in the casualty toll.

However, even the Iraqis made a promising start in the media war when, shortly after invading Kuwait, their leader Saddam Hussein appeared before the world's cameras and, assuming a kindly grin, playfully patted little girls and boys on the head. Turning to joke with a group of women whose families he had taken hostage, he said hostilities would last only a few days and they would become 'heroines of peace'. It was an empty prophecy.

The Gulf War had chutzpah. It made headlines. Though a total of 40,000 British troops and a budget of £1.2 billion were committed to the war effort, it was not considered British enough to be exploited as a propaganda exercise by the Conservative government. It merely helped convince the voters that the recently re-elected prime minister John Major was a 'safe pair of hands'.

The war in Bosnia seems to flare up and fade away at the whims of the news media, some weeks receiving several pages of main news coverage and others nothing at all. However, with the exception of several temporary ceasefires, the conflict has been going on continuously since April, 1992. The war's two main items of news interest are the involvement of British troops and money in a conflict between two European neighbours and the former SDP leader Lord Owen's efforts as a peacemaker.

Terrorists use the news media to put their aggressive messages across. Repeated stories in the media help them demoralize their opponents, gain public sympathy, demonstrate their movements' strengths and create a climate of fear.

Before the 1994 ceasefire, the IRA were masters of news media propaganda, carrying out their bombings on public and bank holidays, as they attracted the most attention. Their favourite locations were such major institutions as the Houses of Parliament, 10 Downing Street, the Bank of England, the Stock Exchange, the Royal Albert Hall, St Paul's Cathedral, the main airports and stations, and the headquarters of large public companies. Their personal targets were public figures such as

Airey Neave, the shadow Conservative Northern Ireland secretary, killed in 1979 as his car was leaving the House of Commons car park, and Lord Mountbatten, first cousin of the Queen, victim of a bomb explosion in 1980 on his yacht while it was moored off Ireland's west coast. Sometimes, to give greater impact, the IRA would telephone the news media just before a bomb was due to go off, its leaders later appearing on air to highlight the power and strength of their movement.

Their tactic of playing on public sympathy was nowhere better demonstrated than the hunger strike by IRA terrorist Bobby Sands in Belfast's Maze prison. The incident created such a stir among the Irish people that it helped Sands to become an Irish MP. Even television documentaries on the imprisonment of the Guildford Four and the Birmingham Six, all of whom, it was later discovered, were wrongly accused of planting IRA bombs, increased public sympathy and emphasized the movement's news media appeal.

The movement's activities reached a peak in 1988, when a spate of attacks was followed by repeated television appearances and newspaper interviews with IRA leaders such as Gerry Adams and Martin McGuinness. The IRA's confidence seemed to increase with each incident as its leaders defended and justified its actions in the media. To curb so blatant a form of propaganda, the government imposed a news media black-out on all reporting of the IRA leaders' views, its aim being, in Mrs Thatcher's words, to 'deprive them of the oxygen of publicity'. However the move became a somewhat hollow farce when the news media exploited a legal loophole and used professional actors to repeat the IRA leaders' views on television news bulletins.

Since the announcement of a ceasefire in 1994, news coverage has concentrated on the progress of peace talks between Sinn Fein and the British and Irish governments and a few isolated acts of aggression.

In terrorism, as in war, it is only the biggest, most public incidents that grab the front pages. After the PLO terrorist Leila Khaled tried to force a New York-bound Israeli plane to divert to Jordan in 1970, she told the press she had acted 'heroically in a cowardly world to prove that the enemy is not invincible'. The same year when hijackers from the Popular Front for the Liberation of Palestine forced down three Arab aircraft on to a deserted airport in Jordan, they not only alerted the news media, but blew the planes up in front of the television cameras.

The main danger facing editors and producers who report on terrorism is that they may unwittingly spread propaganda. In the book, *Terrorism and the Media*, David L Paletz and Alex P Schmid, point out: 'While most editors agree that the media have a responsibility to combat terrorism, they do not seem to realize their complicity with terrorists' goals through their continued coverage of terrorism ... editors must be aware that reporting an event changes that event, that the prominence given to terrorist incidents might increase public fear ... and that media coverage of terrorism could endanger lives.'

Terrorist movements use similar techniques to commercial organizations to promote their causes, calling on the skills of PROs, marketing specialists and press officers to organize press conferences, national rallies, poster campaigns and demonstrations. They also issue educational literature, books and videos as publicity aids. In fact the marketing talents of Sinn Fein's press office has earned it a reputation as the Saatchi and Saatchi of terrorist media departments.

Another form of news media protest is the animal rights movement. The Animal Liberation Front, the most active group, often uses direct confrontation to put its message across. One of the ALF's propaganda tactics is to send letter-bombs and the heads and limbs of animals to MPs and public figures. However, perhaps its most effective tool of protest is to tamper with and contaminate food items in supermarkets. This immediately creates a national alert in the news media, after which the goods are withdrawn and the public warned of the dangers of touching the affected items. Among other methods of media exposure are arson attacks on shops selling animal-tested goods, damaging the homes and personal property of animal scientists, destroying animal-testing equipment in laboratories, and sending press releases and photographs of animals and birds to newspapers after releasing them from battery farms and vivisection centres.

Finally, blood sports such as hunting, shooting and fishing have become major targets of protest in the past two decades. The media-conscious Hunt Saboteurs Association, or Sabs as they are known, ambush well-known hunt meetings to gain maximum coverage, the sight of elegantly-clad huntsmen being toppled off their horses in scenic countryside providing particularly good television footage.

Warring governments and terrorists use the media to demoralize their opponents. It is almost like a second line of resistance. If military tactics or direct aggression fail, then they can fall back on the media's propagandist powers to baffle or mislead their quarries. The news media does not always realize it is being used in a game of blindman's bluff. It is up to sharp-eyed reporters and news editors to thread their way through this subtle media maze in their efforts to produce a readable story.

9

The Investigators

'The press, by pointing out wickedness in high
places, also can cause the wicked to be brought
to grief so that the forces of good may prevail.'

Herbert Altschull, *Agents of Power*

Journalism is about getting the story, whatever the cost. It can
be a prickly process of duping reporters from rival newspapers,
telling lies to gain information from a valuable source or, on a
more personal level, cancelling a dinner date with a new lover.
Many people see reporters as thick-skinned snoopers who
merely ask a few tricky questions before scuttling back to their
newspapers. The average reporter, however, is a presentable
and quick-witted individual with a sharp news sense and an
ability to get hold of the facts and foibles of an event. Some
move on to become investigative reporters, their job being to
unmask the hidden truths behind stories, though the phrase is
occasionally used to describe those reporters who indulge in
sleaze. Today's investigative reporter has a serious role to play
and many have been successful in bringing cases of corruption,
injustice and incompetence into the public eye.

The first modern editor to employ in-depth reporters on a newspaper was Denis Hamilton of the *Sunday Times*. In 1963 he started the newspaper's Insight column. This was a two-page section in which reporters could study the events behind the news, explore topical issues and, if necessary, suggest reforms and changes in the British system. It gave *Sunday Times* readers a bit more to think about than the straightforward reporting of the week's news. Edited by Clive Irving, a former *Sunday Telegraph* feature writer, Insight's first two stories, about the Brain Drain of British scientists to the USA, and why many of the BBC's top executives were joining rival television networks, set the tone for the section.

The 1960s was the era of second-guessing, a wild and permissive time of free thought, experiment and rebellion, and an ideal climate for investigative journalism. A new satire movement was spearheaded by the television show *That Was The Week That Was*, produced by Ned Sherrin. Each week, performers and writers such as Peter Cook, Bernard Levin, Jonathan Miller, Alan Bennett and David Frost mocked politicians, showbiz personalities and public institutions, and helped create an air of irreverence in British society. *Private Eye* magazine, founded by Peter Cook, also turned serious establishment figures into objects of fun, at the same time as earning itself an unending succession of writs.

The era marked the beginning of serious gossip and scandal in Britain. The 1963 Profumo Affair gave the *Sunday Times* Insight team its first real exposé, unravelling the extraordinary life-style of Stephen Ward, the society osteopath and pro-Russian agent, his girlfriend Christine Keeler and the Tory defence minister, John Profumo. As the drama unfolded, the tale of the Cabinet Minister and the Call-girl became a contemporary version of the Prince and the Show-girl. The same year, 1963, also marked the launch of Granada's *World in Action*, a television version of Insight, followed by a catalogue of televisual specials, including Britain's rejection from the Common Market, the rise to power of Labour premier Harold Wilson, and the public tribunal of homosexual spy

William Vassall. *World in Action*'s producers said: 'People these days want to know. The world interests them. They want to be informed. But they want to be informed clearly, thoughtfully and with candour. The cant and the superficial are not good enough.' They saw that British television viewers were bored with discussion programmes chaired by genial hosts, panels of carefully selected experts, and polite but unprovocative comments on daily life. It was time for revelation.

Other television documentaries came to the fore. The founding of *Panorama* in 1953 by BBC talks producer Andrew Miller Jones was a story in itself. One day, during a break in schedules, Jones was looking out of his window on the fifth floor of the BBC's studios at Alexandra Palace. As he gazed at the vista of silhouettes before him, an idea came to him for a programme about new perspectives on life and society. Miller Jones told BBC management who gave the idea their enthusiastic approval and, somewhat aptly, called it *Panorama*. The early editions were anchored by journalist and author Patrick Murphy, and divided into three sections: Matters of the Moment, dealing with topics of the day; Under Fire, which put an expert under the spotlight; and At Random, the forerunner of the investigative programme.

One of *Panorama*'s first presenters was Richard Dimbleby, father of David and Jonathan, whose mellifluous tones accompanied such events as the Queen's coronation, Sir Winston Churchill's memorial service and several post-war general elections. In 1959, Robin Day joined the programme after working as a barrister, his early television duties being as reporter and occasional presenter. By the late 1960s he had developed into a sharp and acerbic interviewer, his spotted bow-tie and rapid wit becoming the scourge of British politicians.

The documentary programme, *This Week*, launched by Associated Rediffusion in 1956 (later taken over by Thames Television), achieved some memorable firsts in the 1960s, including an in-depth study of the links between smoking and lung cancer. Another report, 'Ethiopia – the Unknown Famine', made by Jonathan Dimbleby in 1973, won several television documentary awards and was said to have contributed to the downfall of Ethiopia's dictatorial emperor, Haile Selassie. The programme's most famous investigation, however, was Death on the Rock in 1988. Its evidence about the controversial shooting of three IRA terrorists by the SAS in Gibraltar led to a public outcry, a government inquiry, headed by Lord Windlesham, and several successful libel cases against national newspapers.

Death on the Rock, which the government twice tried to gag, conflicted with a *Sunday Times* Insight report that claimed the IRA terrorists were threatening the SAS, who shot them in retaliation. The programme-makers' view was that two of the terrorists were surrendering to the SAS when they were killed. The controversy prompted Mrs Thatcher to introduce the 1990 Broadcasting Act, reducing some of television's investigative powers and abolishing the Independent Broadcasters' Association. Lord Windlesham said after the inquiry: 'I regard periodic rows between governments of whatever colour and broadcasters as genuine marks – stigmata may be a better word – of a free society.'

The *Sunday Times* Insight column, *This Week* and the early documentaries showed that investigative journalism could challenge the government, institutions and individuals over matters of public interest. More specifically, it had the powers to uncover confidential documents and files that might hide vital information; expose the government's liberal use of Public Interest Immunity Certificates; halt a welter of speculation over the secret activities of politicians and public servants; and help create a more open and honest style of government.

One of the pioneers of the new revelatory style was Duncan Campbell. An Oxford physics graduate, Campbell's early articles in *Time Out* and *New Scientist* earned him a reputation as an exposer of military secrets, two of his most noteworthy scoops being his story about a secret network of tunnels beneath London and his discovery of the Maggiebunker, a nuclear shelter, named after Mrs Thatcher, for government chiefs in Wiltshire.

In his efforts to alert the public about what the government is doing, Campbell has written stories about unauthorized phone-tapping by GCHQ, the government's Cheltenham-based electronic spying centre, and the existence of highly confidential Cold War strategy documents, and in 1977, he was charged under Sections I and II of the Official Secrets Act for writing a *Time Out* article about a British radio spying centre in Cyprus. He was acquitted on the first charge and given an unconditional discharge on the second.

Since 1978, Campbell has written for the *New Statesman* and from 1990 to 1994 was chairman of the magazine's board of directors. His unique gift is his ability to unravel government technical jargon and officialese better than any other journalist of his kind. He is also a discreet operator and highly trusted by his informants, usually receiving his information in anonymous brown packages through the post. Perhaps Campbell's biggest story appeared in the *New Statesman* in 1987 when he revealed that the government was planning a £500 million spy satellite programme named Project Zircon. The government was outraged at this breach of secrecy. However when Campbell defended his story on television, he put up such a spirited case that he has thereafter been referred to as the Lethal Eagle.

As a foreigner, the Australian journalist John Pilger is able to show a detached scorn for the British establishment in his articles. Pilger, who writes for several Fleet Street newspapers and is a respected television commentator, is best known for his reporting of the Vietnam War. While working as a *Daily Mirror* feature writer, Pilger wrote an eleven-page article and a television documentary called 'Year Zero' about the plight of the Cambodians under the Pol Pot and Khmer Rouge regimes. A second documentary, 'Cambodia: The Betrayal' gained him both an Emmy award and an expensive libel action.

During the 1960s and 1970s, Pilger was a key member of the *Daily Mirror*'s investigative team under its editor-in-chief Hugh (later Lord) Cudlipp. Among the shock issues he exposed were the Thalidomide scandal and the state of some of Britain's NHS hospitals. Much of Pilger's campaigning is for victims of injustice, ranging from overworked miners in Britain's industrial north to the plight of Australia's aboriginal children. Like Duncan Campbell he is a fearless forager. His 1983 film, *The Truth Game*, attacking government secrecy over nuclear weapons, made such an impact that the IBA insisted on making another film to give the government version. It prompted journalist Auberon Waugh to introduce the phrase 'to pilger', meaning to unearth or expose, into the British language. Members of the establishment, however, sometimes refer to Pilger, a little unkindly, as the GAW (Great Australian Windbag), while *Private Eye*'s favourite nickname is the Great Bondi Bombshell because of his long fair hair.

Paul Foot is another *enfant terrible* of the British establishment. Educated at Shrewsbury and University College, Oxford, his father was governor of Jamaica and his uncle, Michael Foot, was leader of the Labour Party. After working as an investigative reporter on the *Daily Record* in Glasgow, Foot joined *Private Eye* in 1967 and wrote a column called Footnotes about serious issues of the moment. Five years later he was appointed editor of the *Socialist Worker*, standing, albeit unsuccessfully, as a Socialist Workers' Party candidate.

Much of Foot's journalism is based on left-wing causes and his determined and compassionate defence of several victims of injustice has almost certainly spared them from imprisonment. In the 1960s, he wrote a series of articles calling for the posthumous retrial of James Hanratty, hanged in 1961 after being tried and found guilty of murdering Michael Gregsten on the A6 motorway. Foot's findings were also published in the book *Who Killed Hanratty?* After that, the Thatcherism of the 1980s became his *bête noire*. 'There is poverty, homelessness, sheer unadulterated misery of a kind which would not have been thought of, let alone tolerated, twenty or thirty years ago,' he wrote.

From 1979 until 1994, Foot ran the *Daily Mirror*'s investigations unit, carrying out exposés into the controversial death of Carl Bridgewater at Yew Tree Farm in Wordsley, near Wolverhampton, and the sacking of the Army's Northern Ireland PRO, Colin Wallace, after allegations that he had been involved in a dirty tricks campaign against public figures. When a new regime took over the *Daily Mirror* in 1994, making more than 100 journalists redundant and apparently threatening its left-wing principles, Foot criticized the newspaper's management in his weekly column. When the editor, David Banks, refused to publish it, Foot resigned, rejoining *Private Eye* and continuing where he had left off as writer of the Footnotes column.

Apart from the *Daily Mirror*, the other successful campaigning newspaper during this period was the *Sunday Times*. It continued the traditions of the Insight column under Denis Hamilton's successor, Harold Evans, with stories on phoney wine-labelling, the selling of bogus car insurance policies, and fraudulent antique dealing. The *Sunday Times*'s most famous campaign was a long series of articles in the 1970s on Thalidomide, a sedative drug used during pregnancy, when a team headed by Marjorie Wallace revealed how the babies of several hundred mothers who had taken the drug were born deformed. The articles helped the unfortunate families gain £20 million compensation against Distillers, the parent company of the manufacturers who had marketed the drug in Britain.

In the late 1980s and 1990s, television took over from newspapers as the popular medium for investigations. Watching pictures of events as they actually happened had more impact and excitement than reading about them in the grey columns of newspapers. Television producers began to probe further and to be more adventurous in their film-making, often turning the documentaries into mystery stories or whodunits. Rapid advances in communications made the man-in-the-street more aware of the workings of government and public bodies and the rising number of loopholes that appeared with monotonous regularity in the system. This encouraged producers to spend more time and money on investigations, so that by 1995 there were more than ten serious documentary programmes, ranging from the BBC's *Panorama* and *Newsnight* to Channel 4's *Cutting Edge* and *Dispatches*.

Modern technology has made television films increasingly life-like. The camera's roving eye and its ability to capture people in unguarded moments has given sequences greater edge, enabling interviewers to take a bolder, more ruthless approach to their subjects. Hidden cameras, tape-recorders and microphones add to the suspense as meetings between corrupt businessmen, shady deals and illegal transactions are revealed before the viewer's eye.

Several recent programmes have succeeded in making the government think again on important issues. Investigations into the famous Guildford Four and Birmingham Six trials led to the cases being retried and the defendants acquitted on 'unsafe convictions'; television films about the death of the African activist Steve Biko and the Medellin drugs cartel in Colombia are said to have made at least two governments feel uncomfortable, while a documentary about the Lockerbie air disaster persuaded the government to set up a new inquiry into the facts behind the tragedy.

Investigative journalism has many roles. It can provoke, change laws, bring crooks to justice, and give victims a chance to gain redress. It can also reveal some of the more questionable activities of the news media itself. In 1994, a BBC documentary called *The Tabloid Truth* looked at the workings of a Birmingham news agency. Viewers watched as, in an atmosphere resembling a car auction, reporters and photographers tried to hawk their stories to the national newspapers. In one scene a young reporter, plainly upset that she was unable to extract any comment from the mother of a teenager killed in a road accident, said: 'The only thing I am hoping might break it for us is she's going to the doctor ... to be put on sedatives', while a doorstepping photographer admitted she might have to urinate into a soft drink can so as not to miss taking a picture of the mother of a TV star's mistress. Finally a news agency secretary was persuaded to dress up as a prostitute so that a photographer could take a faked picture of late-night kerb-crawling in Birmingham.

Despite its didactic style, investigative journalism has a humourous side. BBC1's *That's Life*, which was produced and presented by Esther Rantzen on Sunday evenings took a gently humorous and occasionally serious view of the week's events and confidence tricks. If Mrs Mossop, of West Wickham, revealed that £6,000 worth of shining new double-glazed windows had dropped out of their frames, the *That's Life* team went into action, naming the company that installed them, pursuing and grilling their managing director and directors, and often uncovering other cases of negligence by its employees. Sometimes they featured bureaucratic bungles such as an over-zealous council sending out a tax bill for a penny or a company that forwarded someone the same invoice three times. *That's Life* was a combination of consumer guide and watchdog as Miss Rantzen and her team of interviewers roamed the country exposing injustices by crooks and careless companies.

ITV's *The Cook Report* is a sterner, more robust version of *That's Life*, its burly presenter, Roger Cook, pursuing a motley collection of rogues from time share twisters to cowboy plumbers and often getting a short, sharp physical rebuff for his pains. ITV's *Beam and Da Silva* performed a similar, though more light-hearted, role, as its two presenters got evicted from the offices of Soho porn merchants one day and chased by crooked mini-cab drivers the next. BBC1's *Watchdog* programme is a shorter, sharper and more serious investigator of consumer fraud with a stern hands-off message to potential mischief-makers. The merit of these programmes is that they make good television entertainment and help defenceless consumers gain satisfaction for ill treatment.

Crimewatch UK is an investigative programme with a difference. A television equivalent of a police investigation, it uses the medium's unique resources to help solve crimes. By showing secret video films of bank or building society hold-ups and re-enacting crimes using professional actors, it can jog viewers' memories of recent incidents they may have witnessed. The advantage of *Crimewatch* is that, like a police inquiry, it can amass evidence and present it to the viewer, in the same way as a team of detectives would report it to their senior investigating officer. The programme-makers, who work closely with the police, have their own incident desk and a back-up team of police officers and detectives who regularly give evidence and make appeals to the public.

In their efforts to catch criminals the *Crimewatch* presenters also interview victims' friends and families.

Because crime is eminently watchable, especially when shoot-outs and car chases are involved, *Crimewatch UK* is seen by one-fifth of the British viewing public, more than 1,500 viewers regularly phoning its monthly programmes. Since 1983, it has featured 1,350 cases, leading to 300 police convictions and the arrest of 400 potential criminals, but perhaps its greatest achievement was helping to bring to justice Michael Sams, killer of the Leeds teenager Julie Dart in 1991. A special edition of *Crimewatch UK* featured a tape-recording of the suspected killer's voice, which was recognized by Michael Sams's former wife, Susan Oake, who had been watching the programme. She immediately phoned Leeds police and, less than 15 hours later, Sams was arrested and charged with murder.

After Sams's arrest, a reconstruction of the crime called 'A Murderer's Game' was shown by *Crimewatch*. During the film, which used actual witnesses and the police officers involved in the investigation, Miss Oake told viewers: 'I knew immediately it was his voice and I paced up and down 20 or 30 times just shouting: "It's him! It's him!" I felt like I was betraying my children because I knew that this was their father, and it was going to hurt them and it was going to hurt me. But it was something I had to do.'

Today's 'Fleet Street' newspapers deliberately ignore the finely-honed skills of investigative journalism. The middle-market tabloids are more bland and consumer-led than in the past, sacrificing revelatory stories for those with an immediate, less analytical, impact on their readers, while popular tabloid editors regard investigations as too costly, time-consuming and speculative and, more crucially, not saleable enough. Instead they prefer to buy up stories with a guaranteed market. The quality newspapers choose to be less penetrative than they used to be, mainly due to the sizeable resources needed for long-term investigations and the increasing libel risks attached to inaccurate reporting.

The *Daily Mirror*, which carried out many famous exposés, closed its investigative unit when Paul Foot left the newspaper in 1994; while the pioneer of newspaper campaigners, the *Sunday Times*, became more commercial and reactionary in outlook when Murdoch and his editor Andrew Neil took over the newspaper in 1981, concentrating on circulation-boosting splashes, personality profiles and serializations.

Britain has entered the clean, clinical age of the computerized newspaper. Newspapermen are more desk-bound and design-oriented than in the post-war years, while budget-driven executives are rarely prone to speculative whims. It is far easier for a news editor to hand out a showbiz or celeb story that can be telephoned from the office than a vague piece about the training of secret para-military units. Today's newspaper offices are driven by strong proprietors and powerful commercial strategies. It will take a media revolution to change all that.

10

The Techno-Revolution

'In the struggle for freedom of information, technology not politics will be the ultimate decider.'

Arthur C Clarke

Fleet Street's journalists are Britain's back-door spies. They can bug telephones, boardrooms and private houses, use long lenses to probe into embarrassing places, pry into private and public companies, and gain instant access to confidential leaked documents. New technology has given them an unfair advantage over their public. No sooner has a well-known figure committed an indiscretion than a reporter is sending the facts to his newspaper on a portable modem, the story entering the paper's computer system and appearing on the page in minutes. The hapless individual has been zapped with no opportunity to answer back. It is an increasingly common occurrence, for journalists have a formidable array of gadgets at their fingertips that enable them to peer and probe at a moment's notice. No sooner does the rumour machine start rumbling, than the news media's electronic antennae move into action and yet another state secret is exposed to the nation.

The men behind the stories work in open-plan offices filled with visual display units and keyboards where all writing, editing and make-up is carried out on screen. The offices are neat and uncluttered, hardly reminiscent of an information centre filled with news flashes and world-shaking reports. Yet the stories, gossip and scandal are virtually untouched by human hand. They are sent electronically from the computer network to the printing presses and there is scant sign of the traditional newspaperman's tools of pens, paper, rulers, coloured pencils and typewriters.

The British newspaper industry revolution began in 1976 when the *Nottingham Evening Post* used computers to input its news and advertising. One by one, the other provincial newspapers followed suit until a further hi-tec pioneer arrived on the scene in the shape of Eddie Shah. A fourth cousin of the Aga Khan, Shah ran a group of free newspapers in Lancashire and had become increasingly frustrated with the restrictive practices of his print union, the National Graphical Association. So he recruited several non-union printers.

The result was mayhem. The NGA went on strike, picketing Shah's presses and offices in an effort to halt production of his newspapers. But Shah was defiant. 'The pickets will need three armoured tanks, a couple of helicopters with machine-guns and about 600 men from the second parachute regiment to stop the newspapers leaving,' he said. The NGA took no notice and continued to picket. During one bleak Fleet Street weekend they even managed to stop the production of seven national newspapers as they carried on their protest.

On another occasion, 4,000 pickets jostled outside Shah's Warrington headquarters and tried to break down the metal door. Fearing for his life, the worried proprietor telephoned Andrew Neil, editor of the *Sunday Times*. Neil immediately phoned the home secretary Leon Brittan, and asked him to help Shah out. Brittan refused at first, but eventually sent police reinforcements to the scene of the unrest. However when the pickets caught sight of the police in their uniforms, they became violent. A pitched battle broke out between the two factions, barricades collapsed, telegraph poles and wires crashed to the ground and a flurry of missiles of all shapes and sizes flew through the air.

It proved to be the union's last stand. Aided by the police, Shah and his men managed to drive the union pickets back. His victory was to change the course of modern media history. Then Eddie Shah had a dream. During a subsequent meeting, Andrew Neil told Shah about a new seven-day computerized newspaper called *USA Today*. He suggested it might find a niche in the middle, semi-popular sector of the British market. Shah went away and wrote out a list of figures on the back of a cigar packet. They seemed to add up. His next task was to find backers. He approached a number of large companies and eventually raised just over the £20 million he believed he needed to set up the newspaper project. Then he recruited a board of directors for the embryo newspaper. Shah's dream was turning into reality.

In March 1984, he said: 'We're going after an industry that's ripe to be taken. It just needs one guy. After me there will be more and more people doing their own thing. That's when Fleet Street will really feel the pinch.'

At first, Shah's newspaper was dubbed 'The Daily Shah' by a sceptical Fleet Street. Undeterred, he recruited his first editor, Brian MacArthur, editor of the Portsmouth-based *Western Morning News*. Then the couple made a revolutionary announcement. Like the *Nottingham Evening Post* before them, they said reporters and feature writers would input the newspapers' stories straight on to word processors; the stories would be called up by sub-editors on the same system, who would cut them to length, adding headlines and picture captions. They would then be revised by a senior backbench sub-editor. Finally the stories would be allotted to editorial pages made up on computer screens specially designed for page layout. The pages would be electronically cut and pasted together in a matter of minutes.

The two men's next plan was even more ambitious. For news

pictures were to be scanned into computer databases and inserted on the made-up pages at the same time as display and classified advertisements. The finished pages were to be transmitted along cables to three printing plants at Heathrow, Birmingham and Manchester. There they would be turned into plates and printed out into actual pages before rolling off the presses as complete newspapers. Instead of using the rail network to deliver the newspapers nationwide, Shah would use a fleet of delivery vans, so that they could be taken straight to the wholesalers who, in turn, could deliver them to the newsagents and vendors. The newspaper was to be produced by the newly-formed Electrical, Electronic, Telecommunications and Plumbers Union, with a no-strike clause inserted in its members' contracts.

The site chosen for the venture was a large building in Vauxhall Bridge Road, on the borders of Pimlico and Chelsea. The building was renovated; the new equipment installed. Shah and MacArthur then recruited a team of 130 reporters and sub-editors, opting for provincial rather than national journalists, as Shah disliked what he saw as the precious and élitist attitudes of Fleet Street. Shortly before publication day, a brainstorming session was held, in which it was agreed to call the newspaper *Today*, after its American counterpart. On 6 March, 1986, *Today* appeared for the first time, only two hours later than its original deadline. Shah said proudly: 'We have taken a company with untrained people, untrained printers, people who have never seen a newspaper office, journalists who have never been used to working this sort of equipment, and turned it into a newspaper.'

Though it sold 1.25 million copies on that first day, *Today* had a generally poor reception. The colour pictures were too hazy, the typefaces not sharp enough, and the editorial content lacked the impact to stir its readers. Not even glowing pictures of a pregnant Princess of Wales and the engagement photos of Prince Andrew and Sarah Ferguson could restore its rather drab appearance.

As the weeks went by, *Today* began to improve. But it still suffered from under-staffing, its depleted production team often finding it difficult to meet their deadlines. Despite Shah's efforts to keep *Today* buoyant, the newspaper's circulation fell to its break-even figure of 300,000. After all its revolutionary ideas and early commercial promise, Shah's dream was beginning to fade. Disappointed he looked for a new backer. Tiny Rowland's Lonrho agreed to buy 35 per cent of the company, allowing Shah a controlling 51 per cent. Yet still *Today*'s fortunes continued to waver and 12 months later it was sold to Rupert Murdoch.

Despite the newspaper's faltering start, Shah had achieved a major breakthrough in British journalism – the launching of Britain's first national computerized newspaper. He had succeeded in breaking the stranglehold of the print unions, whose closed-shop policies and restrictive practices had made British newspaper production too wasteful and costly, problems that had originally been highlighted by a team of management consultants from the Economist Intelligence Unit and the 1977 Royal Commission on the Press.

Meanwhile, Andreas Whittam Smith started making plans for his own national newspaper, the *Independent*. His idea had three main merits. First, he could use cost-effective printing – hiring a regional evening newspaper's presses while they were idle rather than building a costly new print works. Second, he could take advantage of the new labour-saving technology introduced by *Today*. Third, there was a noticeable gap in the newspaper readership market between the *Daily Telegraph* and *The Times*.

Whittam Smith enlisted the help of two *Telegraph* colleagues, Matthew Symonds, who wrote economics leaders, and feature writer Stephen Glover. For the next six months, the three men worked on their secret strategy. Sometimes when they made discreet job offers to close colleagues, they got a sceptical response. Even the founders themselves had occasional misgivings about taking on a major project without any direct business experience. However they managed to keep it under wraps until 22 December 1985, when the *Sunday Times* reported that a 'mysterious band of newspaper editors and executives are trying to raise capital in the city', followed by a story in the *Financial Times* five days later revealing the names of the three founders.

Now that their plans were public knowledge, the trio resigned from their jobs at the *Telegraph*, and moved into a suite of offices in London Wall. For the first time, they could give the newspaper their undivided attention. When they asked the advertising agency, Saatchi and Saatchi, to carry out a market research survey into the *Independent*'s chances of success, the findings were most encouraging. It seemed there was a significant gap in the AB1 and AB2 readership market for a serious newspaper. Next, they asked Saatchis to test market six possible titles – the Examiner, Chronicle, Arena, Nation, Twenty-Four Hours and the Independent. From a 500-name poll of newspaper readers, the *Independent* came first with 64 per cent of the votes, just ahead of the Examiner, with 63 per cent. The *Independent*'s newly appointed advertising director, Adrian O'Neill, commented: 'All our research has shown that our independence is a very important factor, so we are going to be single-minded and make sure people know we are financially independent, intellectually independent, editorially independent and politically independent.' Hence Saatchis' confident slogan: 'It is. Are you?'

In January, 1986, the *Independent*'s founders had a stroke of fortune. The printing dispute at Murdoch's national newspapers in Wapping had begun. It meant that for 12 months, two of the *Independent*'s rivals, *The Times* and *Sunday Times* would not be published, giving the newspaper an unexpected supply of new readers, and prompting many frustrated Wapping journalists to apply for jobs. It enabled the founders to take on several big-name writers to adorn the *Independent*'s future pages.

Now, Whittam Smith and his two co-founders faced perhaps their hardest task of all – raising capital. The risks attached to backing a computerized quality newspaper seemed almost insurmountable to most City investors, however after months of hard, unstinting negotiations, Whittam Smith managed to persuade 30 companies to put a total of £18 million into the *Independent*'s holding company, Newspaper Publishing plc.

The guiding principle behind the *Independent* was that, unlike any other Fleet Street newspaper, no investor was allowed to own more than ten per cent of its shares. This minority holding policy gave the newspaper genuine independence. However, to the founders' chagrin, they later discovered that the tycoon Robert Maxwell, owner of the Mirror group, had secretly bought a 4.81 per cent holding through a north of England financial services company called Lancashire and Yorkshire. However its ten per cent rule safeguarded the company from the Czech entrepreneur's notorious acquisition tendencies.

The founders' next obstacle was more technical than financial. Like any other marketable product, the *Independent* needed to be eye-catching to attract its punters, the readers, and enticing enough to make them read on beyond the first page. Several Fleet Street designers were recruited. The newspaper's appearance, they decided, would be simple but classical, the typefaces unfussy and the layout symmetrical, and the average story should be slightly longer than the *Daily Telegraph*'s. Having set the tone of the newspaper, the founders and their co-directors moved into new premises in City Road and installed the computer software and hardware, including electronic page make-up screens and Datrax laser-scanning equipment that could fax pages of editorial and advertising plus colour pictures to the printing presses.

Then a more human problem arose. The newspaper's journalists had never used computers before, and some of them suffered from technophobia – a fear of electronic machinery – visibly shaking at the prospect of having to work on word processors instead of typewriters. It took them weeks, in some cases months, before they were able to master the new inputting techniques – aided by a team of computer experts. Even then a few of them experienced panic attacks as they tried to grapple with their computers' complexities.

In the run-up to the launch, dummies of the newspaper were scrutinized daily by members of the production team. Despite his lack of layout experience, Whittam Smith usually had the last word, sending each dummy back for a final re-jig until, six weeks later, the final working sample was produced. He was particularly pleased when a picture of a golden eagle with a newspaper in its talons that had been drawn by one of the designers, landed on his desk one day. It was to become the *Independent*'s logo.

The marketing continued apace. Three million leaflets, bearing a cryptic message from Whittam Smith, were delivered to selected homes throughout Britain. 'During more than 20 years in Fleet Street, I watched the deterioration in national newspapers. Appalling labour problems and corrosive management policies made progress a hopeless prospect. We prize even-handed reporting and good writing. Accuracy, clarity, wit – these are the qualities we ask of our journalists,' he said.

It was agreed that Whittam Smith should edit the newspaper, with Symonds his deputy and Glover assistant editor (foreign news). The founders were happy with the pecking order, as that was the order in which they had joined the project. The die was cast. On 6 October 1986, the first edition of the *Independent* entered 650,000 British homes. Apart from a slight technical hitch on a colour page at the Sittingbourne print works, it was a model launch. Appearing on television that evening, Whittam Smith said his team was 'free to make up our own minds on policy issues, to expose commercial skulduggery and to query the establishment, however broadly defined, whether of left or right. We will both praise and criticize without reference to a party line.'

Max Hastings, then editor of the *Daily Telegraph*, commented somewhat prophetically, in view of the newspaper's later troubles: 'It's a respectable, honourable, responsible, pretty dull newspaper. It lacks humour. It will survive. When it has its financial crisis, some rich sugar-daddy will come along and rescue it.' The *Guardian*'s editor Peter Preston said: 'They need to offer something absolutely different. This is absolutely the same.'

Distinctive and clean-looking, the *Independent* was well received by the chattering classes and most of the main city institutions. During the newspaper's first week, it sold more than 500,000 copies a day, eventually settling into a more steady 350,000 to 400,000. Unlike *Today* it had few production or distribution problems. It also managed to secure a manageable level of advertising. Several of its competitors were still dubious about its survival in a cut-throat market, however, arguing that when *The Times* and *Sunday Times* went back into production it would be seriously threatened.

In its first 12 months, figures showed that the *Independent* was taking sizeable chunks of readers from its rivals, the *Daily Telegraph* and *Guardian*. Readers liked its clarity and good picture quality. The news media establishment also gave it their approval. It was voted Newspaper of the Year by Granada television's *What the Papers Say*, won the Hopkinson award for photo-journalism and the best newspaper award in the Newspaper Design Awards.

By the end of 1987, editorial spending was higher than anticipated. Whittam Smith asked all journalists to be strict with their expenses claims and banned all freebies – the free holidays and trips that are an accepted perk of Fleet Street. He then told them to put a motto above their desks: 'No profits. No Independence.' When editorial spending began to seriously exceed its targets, all journalists' pay rises were frozen and no new staff taken on. Finally the newspaper managed to attract more investment by raising its shareholding limit from 10 to 15 per cent.

Then Whittam Smith made perhaps his biggest mistake. After watching another newspaper, the *Sunday Correspondent*, enter the market, he decided to launch a Sunday version of the *Independent* as a spoiling operation. The *Independent on Sunday* was launched in January 1990, with Stephen Glover as its editor. At first its circulation topped 700,000, then it began to dwindle, eventually falling to around 300,000. Though the new *Independent* succeeded in pushing out the *Sunday Correspondent* – dubbed the Sunday Despondent by *Private*

Eye – it had made a loss of £8 million by the end of the year. Advertising revenue was also falling on the daily as the advertisers were not confident enough of the newspapers' long-term futures.

The founders approached two European newspapers, the Italian *La Repubblica* and the Spanish *El Pais*. Both agreed to buy a 14.9 per cent shareholding in Newspaper Publishing plc which raised £21.5 million. They also made 56 people redundant in editorial and non-editorial posts and tried to merge the two newspapers into a seven-day operation. But the idea did not catch on due to the differing markets of a weekly and a daily newspaper. Then in May 1991, Glover resigned as editor of the Sunday, later severing his connection with the company altogether. In his book *Paper Dreams*, he said of the *IoS*: 'It was not greeted as a journalistic triumph. The world had expected that we would launch with the confidence of a batsman who comes to the crease having already made a hundred, and instantly take on the authority of the *Independent*.'

Between 1992 and 1994, the circulation of both newspapers fell, staff turnover was high, advertising revenue continued to fall, and one by one the big-name writers left for more prosperous rivals. Murdoch's price war further reduced the daily *Independent*'s readership and even a complete revamp of its design could not change its fortunes. Facing serious financial trouble, the two newspapers looked for new backers. Much to Fleet Street's and all other members of the news media's surprise, a majority shareholding was bought by the comparatively downmarket Mirror Group Newspapers in March 1994. Newspaper Publishing's survival was guaranteed but its glory days had gone.

The two *Independent*s were victims of their own ambitions. After starting with a successful formula, their founders over-reached themselves by launching a Sunday newspaper. Not even stricter budgetary controls could save the newspapers from the harshness of the recession and the Fleet Street price war. Several other hi-tec newspapers, the *London Daily News*,

News on Sunday and the *Post*, tried to repeat the *Independent* and *Today* formulae but failed. Colin Seymour-Ure says in *The British Press and Broadcasting Since 1945*: 'Independence, like party ownership of papers, belonged to an earlier age of smaller self-contained organizations. Its logic remained intact, and new life was indeed breathed into it by the *Independent*. But it was necessarily precarious in practice, for it depended on financial security.'

Though *Today* and the *Independent* were pioneers of national computerization, it was Rupert Murdoch's audacity that forced the rest of Fleet Street to adopt new technology. After secretly building a £66 million plant at Wapping, he recruited members of the newly-formed EEPTU to operate his new equipment, persuading the journalists on his five newspapers, nearly all of whom were members of the National Union of Journalists, to move into the new offices. The rest of Britain's nationals realized they would have to follow suit, if they were to compete in an increasingly costly and labour-intensive market. So for the next three years, Fleet Street went hi-tec, introducing new technology, making thousands of printers redundant, replacing rail distribution with fleets of modern delivery vans, and, in some cases, moving to more economical premises in east London.

Today's national newspaper is designer-led, its headlines bolder, its pictures bigger and its stories more dramatic than its over-manned predecessor. It appears in multi-coloured sections and relies on a greater output of stories than before. Its sub-editors are capable technicians, many of them working unhealthily long hours to keep up with the changes they have to master. Traditional newspaper artists, who took great pride in their page layouts, have been replaced by subs doubling as designers, their role being to lay out pages with geometric precision on computer screens. It will not be long before voice activators replace computers in newspaper production and streamline the process even further.

Newspapers are designed to woo readers. Both the popular and quality press present their news stories so as to create maximum impact, while features are soft in appearance, with elegant typefaces and imaginative use of white space. Frequent use of colour – even on scenes of violence, war and crime – helps to caress the most jaundiced of eyes. Whereas the serious Sunday newspapers provide arts and culture sections for their more reflective readers, the dailies carry supplements on a variety of interests ranging from education to health. Magazines and TV listings sections also add to their entertainment value. The reader-in-a-hurry can even call up *The Times* and *Daily Telegraph* on the Internet, reading items of the day's news, business, arts and sport at the press of a button.

Michael Crozier, designer of the *Independent*, says in his book *The Making of the Independent*: 'Journalists ... have less knowledge of how it is done than at any time in history. It was comparatively easy to understand how an old-fashioned Linotype machine operated and how a page was assembled and printed. Such is modern technology that few, apart from a technological élite, can begin to understand the inner workings of a computer or facsimile transmitter. The workings of the "new tech" revolution are a mystery to most people.' They may be a mystery to today's journalists, but let us hope their basic grasp of the English language continues to shine through the maze of electronic innovation.

11

The Vice of the People

'The dignity of a journalist is reduced when he is
asked to intrude into the private affairs, and in
particular the private grief, of others, or to twist
his own honest view of a story to suit a political
view or any other language.'

Lord Kemsley

News is an addictive drug the British cannot resist. Whether
tuning in to the radio or television or glancing at a newspaper,
the public faces a daily siege of information. We have become a
nation of news carriers, gathering morsels and half-morsels at
every turn; participants in a game of knowledge and expertise.
It can be fun to reveal the dirty deeds of Lady McDrummond in
the local pub, or, in a more reflective mood, to discuss recent
troop movements in Bosnia-Herzegovina. Whatever we read,
hear or see, from the workings of parliament to the antics of a
fallen actress, news helps us to know our place in the world and
to feed our fantasies about life, money, and success. However
there is another more worrying side to the information factory.

135

We tend to believe almost everything we read or hear, as we have no means of contradicting it. Each day we are the unwitting victims of propaganda, half-truths, make-believe, stories that are hyped up and facts that are deliberately designed to mislead. We may be better informed, but we are also becoming the innocent pawns of the news media.

A classic example of media-speak occurred when pop-star Michael Jackson, who had stopped off in Dublin during a world tour, was asked to do a photo-call by the *Daily Mirror*. At the last minute, the newspaper found that Jackson had mistakenly left his pet chimpanzee, Bubbles, in New York. Knowing the pet was an important part of his act, the *Mirror* dispatched a handler to find another monkey at Dublin zoo. After choosing a likely-looking replacement, the handler took it back to his house ready for the photo-call with Jackson, putting the chimpanzee in the kitchen with a bowl of food. When the handler returned that evening, he found a large crowd had gathered outside his house and, looking up, saw the chimp swinging from one of the rafters under the roof. In his haste, he had forgotten to lock the kitchen door, and the chimp had escaped. That night the handler put the chimp in a spare-room, this time remembering to lock the door, and the photo-call went ahead as planned the next day.

Too much of today's news is made up. Newspapers produce stories that are little more than promotional stunts to catch the eye of the reader and to fill the growing number of pages they carry. Today's popular tabloid sub-editors often double as Mayfair copywriters, using verbal gimmickry to weave a spell of fantasy round their pictures and stories. Readers of the more lurid tabloids could be forgiven for thinking they are spectators in a world of make-believe where cars regularly drop from skyscrapers, double-decker buses are discovered at the North Pole, boyfriends fly through windows with boxes of chocolates, and every pop-star has a pet monkey. Even television and radio news bulletins like to lead with tabloid-style stories to attract the attention of their viewers and listeners. Yet, unless we resort to truth monitors or the psychics that the news media is so fond of promoting, how do we know whether this story or that is true? Despite the myriad sources of information around us, we live in a void of ignorance.

There are also more sinister forces at work. The information superhighway, on which news desks depend for many of their stories, masks any number of vested interests. As we have seen, these can range from terrorist propaganda to the half-truths of a spying network, the commercial cunning of private enterprise to the devious ploys of hoaxers. Most journalists have an inbuilt scepticism and are trained to check and double-check their sources. However they cannot pick up on all the facts, figures and statements that seep into their offices.

The speed and frequency of deadlines means that, instead of meeting their sources face-to-face, an increasing number of today's reporters and correspondents rely on mobile and standard telephones, faxes, pagers, teleprinters and computers to get their stories. This creates an artificial barrier between the newsmen and the news, leading to errors, misunderstandings and reports that lack the inimitable freshness of human contact. By the time the finished product has been revised and re-written by several sub-editors, much of its basic elements may have been lost in the telling.

It is similar to a story that is running the rounds of a local street. By the time it has reached the eighth house, much of its meaning has usually been altered or lost. Even the sixteenth-century's national news service, which consisted of innkeepers passing on information between inns and post-houses, was not infallible. Sometimes the news, which was carried on horseback by young post-boys, had changed out of all recognition after about 100 miles. In time, the messenger network became so popular that the information was written down in newsletters, one of which became Britain's first newspaper, *The Weekly News*, in 1622. It would be interesting to know what a *Weekly News* reporter might think of today's news networks.

Members of today's news media are street-wise operators who constantly strive to keep ahead of their rival newspapers, radio stations and television networks. To do so, they have to resort to evermore far-fetched gimmicks such as bingo, prize draws, holidays – and hyped-up news stories. Newspapers and other media outlets play the same games as commercial companies. Just as industry has to resort to ingenious and sophisticated methods to sell its goods and services, so does the media when it is selling on news and information.

Whereas industry sells tangible benefits, the news media is a dispenser of knowledge. And knowledge means power. The problem is that the media does not use its power responsibly. A little colour, opinion and poetic licence is sometimes needed in stories. The public would soon lose interest if the news was presented as a series of dull, unadorned facts. However many events are dramatic and stirring enough to stand up on their own merits and do not need media hype to give them impact. Even human interest stories do not have to be embellished with exaggeration and hyperbole to make them readable.

The main culprits are the proprietors. Owners of newspapers and television networks are men of influence, signing multi-million pound deals and controlling complex empires. Their cultivation of politicians, statesmen, and international leaders gives them urbanity and a rare insight into world events. Yet in their pursuit of power and self-interest they are unwilling to analyse the consequences of their actions and the output of their interests. They may not even notice that much of the information they are selling is both harmful and debasing.

The next culprits are the alchemists of the day's news – the editors and programme producers. They face a range of pressures such as the wishes of their proprietors, the need to maintain viewing and circulation figures, government interference and their own job security. They have to be able to outwit the opposition by the clever use of colour stories and exclusives or, on a more basic level, sleaze, and must vet each main story as it goes to press. Too many of their editorial decisions are tempered by the group's vested interests in, say, West Africa, friends in high places and big business.

The third culprits are the reporters, correspondents and

photographers. As we have seen, tabloid journalists take it for granted that names and addresses have to be made up, that they must lie and cheat to gain information, flannel unashamedly to get a winning line out of a source, and pry unashamedly into people's private lives and moments of grief in their pursuit of a saleable story or photograph. Sometimes their snooping involves the handing over of large sums of money. However if a reporter should so much as dare to take a moral stance, he faces losing his job. Not surprisingly many of them assume a cynical veneer to hide their real feelings about their daily dirty work. Even serious reporters who are trying to write plausible and well-argued copy, sometimes find it difficult to write a sensible story because of the pressures put on them by news editors, editors and proprietors.

Finally, the victims of the news media are the general public. Our senses, standards and beliefs have become dulled by a constant flow of hype and propaganda, making us less able to tell right from wrong and good behaviour from bad. As our critical faculties have been blunted, we have become less discerning, less able to tell fact from fiction and genuine style from gauche vulgarity. The daily output of news has turned us into androids floating in a man-made vacuum. Each day we look on helplessly as another politician, bishop, judge, member of the royal family or famous film-star is humiliated. Government scandals, companies making promises to their customers that they do not fulfil, swindling insurance companies and bogus charities all add to our general bewilderment about the society we live in.

It is only human to experience a certain smugness when reading or hearing about others' misfortunes, but not when such stories become a national obsession. Neither do we gain any satisfaction from constantly hearing about a violent, ecstasy-aided culture and the mind-blowing tales of teenage killers and drug freaks. Not content to give us an unbiased version of the day's events, the news media sometimes seems intent on drawing us into a world of one-upmanship and envy, in which it is normal to quarrel with our nearest and dearest and to covet the lifestyles of our neighbours and friends. Too many modern newspapers take a sadistic delight in shaming the famous, undermining them until they plead for mercy — or threaten libel suits.

Just who can we turn to to lead us through this amoral maze? At present, the news media sets its own standards and has no independent authority to measure just how far from the truth it is straying. The Press and Broadcasting Complaints Commissions are non-statutory bodies with limited powers of censorship. One alternative might be a Ministry of Information similar to those used in the First and Second World Wars. However such a measure would need all-party support to survive successive governments and might lead to accusations of censorship by the news media itself. A second option could be an institute of fine minds able to direct our reading, viewing and listening habits, though such a body might be dismissed as élitist and authoritarian.

The task of monitoring the media is an imponderable that so far no one is willing to tackle. First, the government is as reluctant to impose curbs on the news media's powers as the media is to accept them. Second, governments are loath to regulate an aspect of national life that can often be encouraged to do their bidding. Third, they do not wish to be accused of behaving like autocrats or to upset the large pro-freedom of the press lobby. Naturally governments fear too much revelation by the news media but they also concede that genuine disclosure is one of the benefits of a free press. They know a news media with a reasonably open brief can keep a permanent check on the excesses of governments and oppositions, public bodies and businesses, and charities and crooks, bringing discrepancies to the notice of the public and helping to prevent them recurring.

Britain prides itself on its freedom of the press. However there have been three recent examples of the government trying to change the rules. In 1984, Sarah Tisdall, a Ministry of Defence clerk, told the *Guardian* that the government was about to massage public opinion about the siting of Britain's first Cruise missile. As a result she was prosecuted under the Official Secrets Act. However the Labour opposition and all advocates of a free press said the leak was in the public interest, pointing out that if the government truly believed in democracy it would have taken no action. Miss Tisdall was sent to prison.

The same year, Clive Ponting, an MoD executive officer, was prosecuted for leaking classified information when he told Labour MP Tam Dalyell the true story of the sinking of the *Belgrano*, that the ship was in fact sailing away from the British fleet not towards it when it was torpedoed, as Mrs Thatcher had claimed at the time. The case against him, which received extensive news media coverage, was eventually dismissed by the High Court Jury. But it was another example of the government using an alleged breach of national security to try to save itself from an embarrassing situation.

The following year, the Conservative government fought even harder to gag democracy. Peter Wright, a former MI5 officer, wrote a book called *Spycatcher* about his work and experiences in the secret service, first publishing it in Australia and later bringing it out in the USA. As a result many copies were shipped back to Britain and sold over the counter. The book was also serialized in the *Sunday Times*. Although the memoirs contained few revelations, apart from a secret services plot to discredit Harold Wilson between 1974 and 1976, the government used High Court injunctions to halt further newspaper extracts until 1987. Lord Bridge, a leading British law lord, said at the time: 'Freedom of speech is always the first casualty under a totalitarian regime ... the present attempt to insulate the public in this country from information which is freely available elsewhere is a significant step down that very dangerous road.'

The delicate balance between censorship and disclosure exists in all countries with a democratic style of government. One of the strongest arguments for a free, uninhibited press is a Freedom of Information Act. The United States introduced one in 1966, shortly followed by the Commonwealth countries, Australia, New Zealand and Canada. By giving the news media greater access to information, such an Act is meant to ensure there is an effective check on the government and major institutions. It is doubtful, however, whether the relentless scavenging of its tabloids has given the average American greater peace of mind than his British counterpart.

A British Freedom of Information Act would certainly open up many secret government and industry files, but with the government's tradition for secrecy, it would almost certainly be accompanied by a new privacy law or press tribunal headed by a judge. Instead of making the workings of government and important bodies more open and accountable, it would create a new set of obstacles for the news media and the general public.

At present, the British government's strongest weapon against news media disclosure is the Official Secrets Act. Upset by their failure to prevent widespread publicity over the Tisdall, Ponting and *Spycatcher* cases, the Conservative government introduced a revised version of the 1911 Act in 1989. Though it permitted the release of information on subjects that did not pose a threat to national security, it made it illegal for anyone to release unofficial information on defence, security, the intelligence services, facts leading to the committing of a crime, international relations, and interception. In an effort to prevent a repeat of *Spycatcher*, the new Act said any classified material published overseas could not be released in Britain.

Soon after the Act, Fleet Street's reputation sank lower than at any other time this century. An increasing number of tabloid sensations had been upsetting and harming people in public life, causing pleas for censure in parliament and critical leaders in the serious newspapers and television programmes. Several editors had been discussing the problem among themselves, but were unwilling to make a public stand. The government, too, was reluctant to take action, despite the efforts of two MPs, Tony Worthington (Labour) and John Browne (Conservative) to introduce privacy bills in 1989. Though, somewhat ironically, Browne later lost his seat after news media revelations about his marriage and business affairs. Several previous attempts by MPs to introduce bills were also overturned, starting with two at the turn of the century which were foiled by media owners' links with cabinet ministers, while Labour MP Brian Walden's Privacy Bill in 1970 and Anne Clwyd's Right of Reply Bill in 1987 were rejected during their first and second readings respectively in the House of Commons. The pro-freedom lobbies had won the day.

It was left to the editor of the *Independent* to take the initiative. In 1989, Andreas Whittam Smith called a meeting of Fleet Street's editors. His aim was twofold. To control the rising tide of tabloid sleaze and to prevent further examples of government censorship such as Official Secrets Acts. A sub-committee of editors, chaired by Whittam Smith, was formed. They were Bernard Shrimsley, former editor of the *News of the World*, Brian MacArthur, founding editor of *Today*, and Sir Frank Rogers, deputy chairman of the Newspaper Publishers Association.

The editors agreed to draw up a voluntary code of practice to show the government and the British establishment they were willing to take responsibility for their actions. After gaining the backing of Fleet Street's most powerful proprietors, Murdoch and Maxwell, the editors held a five-hour meeting at London's World Trade Centre in December 1989, where they drafted the new code. Its main aims were to prevent invasion of privacy when it was not in the public interest, to appoint ombudsmen, or readers' representatives, on all national newspapers, to keep a check on complaints from those who felt aggrieved by stories, and to ensure that all mistakes in newspapers were corrected.

The code of practice was a clever compromise. By agreeing to regulate their own industry, editors helped reassure the establishment and the man-in-the-street about their future behaviour. In 1990, the government too showed its concern about the lowering of journalistic standards when it asked the Home Minister Tim Renton to set up a public inquiry into the news media. Called the Calcutt Committee after its chairman, David Calcutt, a barrister and master of Magdalene College, Cambridge, its members consisted of two lawyers, David Eady and John Spencer; John Cartwright, the SDP president and MP for Woolwich; journalists Simon Jenkins and Sheila Black; and John Last, director of the Charities Trust and a former member of the Press Council.

The Calcutt Committee was also known as the Frugal Committee because of the small portions of sandwiches and coffee that were handed round during its meetings in a Home Office building near Goodge Street tube station. Later the committee travelled once a month to Calcutt's workplace at Magdalene College where the meetings, which were held over £8-a-head government issue lunches, were long and generally inconclusive. Its report concluded: 'We have found no reliable evidence to show whether unwarranted intrusion into individual privacy has or has not arisen over the last 20 years,' though it added: 'The past two decades have seen changes in the character of the tabloid market, with a degree of competition not present since the pre-war circulation battles ... This may have led some tabloid editors to feel "let off the leash" and to become too intrusive in pursuit of competitive advantage.'

The committee made a unique proposal. It said the commission should have its own 24-hour hotline for the benefit of public figures or members of the public who thought their privacy was about to be invaded. The commission could then contact the editor of the relevant newspaper or newspapers and warn him that the code was about to be breached, though it would be unable to prevent actual publication. The committee also recommended that the Press Council, which was set up in 1953 as Britain's only officially recognized defender of press freedom, should be abolished and replaced by a Press Complaints Commission. The commission, said the committee, was a final warning to the news media to raise its standards. If newspapers continued to intrude and annoy, a press complaints tribunal, headed by a judge, would be set up with established powers to prosecute offending newspapers and journalists.

However, the government was still reluctant to take a firm stand against the media, for when the commission was set up on 1 January, 1991, it put in an eight-hour helpline – instead of a 24-hour hotline – so that those who thought their privacy was about to be invaded could discuss their problems with a commission member. Editors would only be contacted in extreme circumstances. Under the chairmanship of Lord McGregor of Durris, former chairman of the 1977 Royal Commission on the Press, it had 16 members, including public figures, businessmen and three journalists, *Daily Star* editor Brian Hitchen, *News of the World* editor Patsy Chapman and *Daily Telegraph* editor Max Hastings.

The commission approved the idea of ombudsmen on individual titles, while the editor's voluntary code of practice was adopted as the official code of the newspaper industry. At the same time, a number of new clauses were added. It became a criminal offence for newspapers to pry into people's homes and gardens, hotel rooms and hospital wards when it was not in the public interest; it banned payments for articles written by criminals, their relations and friends or witnesses in criminal cases; it ordered newspapers to avoid all forms of discrimination; forbade the harassing of accident victims and those suffering from personal grief; banned the seeking of information by intimidation, the interviewing of children under the age of 16 without their parents' permission, and the use of privileged financial information for journalists' own profit; finally it banned the use of hidden listening devices and the interception of telephone calls unless it was in the public interest.

The new Press Complaints Commission gave newspapers their first serious taste of self-regulation. The danger was that, despite a very minor softening of their powers, editors could still pry and probe, knowing they would be criticized but not prosecuted. Two early examples of the commission's frailty occurred when it was asked to rule against one of its own members, Patsy Chapman, editor of the *News of the World*, about a case of intrusion into the private life of Labour MP Clare Short. Though Ms Chapman agreed to print the commission's ruling, she refused to make a public apology to the MP. The other complaint was made by Prince Andrew who was so upset by several pictures in the *People* of his daughter Eugenie running around naked in the garden of his home that he reported it to the commission. It decided that the newspaper had breached the code on two counts – the pictures did not have the Princess's parents consent and were taken with a long lens on to private property. However instead of publishing its ruling, the *People*'s owner Robert Maxwell and editor Bill Hagerty ran a story criticizing the commission and accusing it of threatening national newspapers.

Since then the commission has been taken more seriously. Its rulings have been discussed in parliament and by an establishment consistently ruffled by the powers of the news media. It is also given responsible coverage in both the quality and popular newspapers and on radio and television. Ironically, in the four years since it was set up, the commission has witnessed the worst and most prolonged spell of media sleaze in British history, even surpassing the much-reported scandals and indiscretions of George IV and his courtiers. Politician after politician has been toppled, every member of the royal family with the exception of the Queen Mother has been attacked, and nearly every week a public personality has had to seek legal recourse, resulting in a number of notable libel settlements against national newspapers.

In 1993, there was another attempt to introduce legislation when the National Heritage Secretary David Mellor drew up plans for tighter press laws in public life. But, like the unfortunate John Browne, Mellor too became a victim of media exposure when the press published details of his affair with the actress Antonia de Sancha. As a result his ministerial career was cut short and his ideas had to be abandoned. Later that year, Labour MP Clive Soley introduced a Freedom and Responsibility of the Press Bill. Although it passed its first and second readings, the proposed law faltered at the committee stage in the House of Commons. Once again the idea of a privacy bill became a popular topic of debate rather than a serious option on the floor of the House of Commons. But the sleaze carried on regardless.

One of the worst examples occurred in 1994 when sneak photographs were taken of the Princess of Wales exercising in a west London gym. The pictures, published in the *Daily* and *Sunday Mirror*, caused outrage among the majority of the public. Even rival tabloid editors expressed surprise at such an intimate incursion into the life of a royal. The incident prompted the commission to appoint a privacy commissioner, Robert Pinker, a London School of Economics professor. He was called into action almost immediately when a *Mail on Sunday* reporter, posing as a cripple, managed to stay in the home of writer Germaine Greer. The reporter, Peter Hennessy, had responded to an article in the *Big Issue* in which Ms Greer offered to take in anyone who was homeless or down on their luck. After his brief stay, Hennessy wrote about his experience in the *Mail on Sunday*. Pinker said Hennessy and the newspaper had breached the industry's code by using subterfuge and invasion of privacy in pursuit of a story.

Pinker was also given special powers to report serious privacy abuses to proprietors. He put these into effect when the *News of the World* published pictures of a wan and frail-looking Countess Spencer in the gardens of a private health clinic. After receiving a complaint from Viscount Spencer, Pinker contacted the *News of the World*'s owner Rupert Murdoch, who publicly reprimanded the newspaper's editor, Piers Morgan. Since then, the government's Heritage Committee has rejected the idea of media legislation. Instead, it has recommended a 24-hour hotline – as proposed by the Calcutt Committee – and a compensation fund for privacy victims.

How long will the government and the establishment tolerate the indiscretions of the news media? At present, it is seen as a valuable tool by the Conservative government, especially when it is facing electoral difficulties and political crises. Even though it continues to embarrass, upset and push politicians out of their jobs, the media's propaganda value seems to outweigh the effects of its disruptive powers.

For now, the news media will continue to participate in a

consumer-led society riddled with promotions, gimmickry and speculation. Our hearts will continue to go out to people falling off their polo ponies or down the sides of mountains, and to victims of plane crashes and Far East earthquakes; we will gain smug satisfaction from reading about actors having flings with prostitutes and pop-stars being caught in bed with their chauffeurs; and an increasing number of genuine news stories will be replaced by gossip and tittle-tattle that appeals to the senses rather than the sensibilities.

Newspapers will carry on printing without recourse to market research or readership surveys to find out what their public really wants. They will continue to sell fantasy, so long as sales remain buoyant, the advertisers respond in kind and journalists, editors and proprietors get a thrill out of plying their curious trade. Newspapermen will continue to show off to their rivals on other newspapers, to be expert on everything when they know little about anything, to fall asleep on the job, fiddle their expenses, tell VIPs they are from *The Times* when they really work for the *Sun*, curry favour with influential politicians, doorstep the homes of mistresses, film stars, princesses and vagabonds, send Christmas parcels to high commissioners they have never met and play outrageous hoaxes on their colleagues.

As leisure-time increases and life becomes faster, the British public, will spend more and more time reading newspapers and enjoying radio and television bulletins, satisfying its curiosity about the latest gossip, the day's events and the problems of the world. Such diversions help us to relieve the tedium of a dull week and provide lively conversational topics for family and friends. Each day we will continue to absorb this rising tide of information, unaware of the dubious forces behind it, forces that can alter our attitudes, lower our standards, influence our relationships, and even damage our health. The British news media has become the vice, rather than the voice, of the people.

Bibliography

Baistow, Tom, *Fourth Rate Estate: An Anatomy of Fleet Street*, Canada Publishing, 1985.

Bower, Tom, *Maxwell: The Outsider*, Mandarin, 1992.

Chippindale, Peter and Horrie, Chris, *Stick it Up Your Punter*, Heinemann, 1990.

Cockerell, Michael, Hennessy, Peter and Walker, David, *Sources Close to the Prime Minister*, Macmillan, 1984.

Coleridge, Nicholas, *Paper Tigers*, Heinemann, 1991.

Crozier, Michael, *The Making of the* Independent, Gordon Fraser, 1990.

Cumings, Bruce, *War and Television*, Verso, 1992.

Curran, James and Seaton, Jean, *Power Without Responsibility*, Routledge, 1993.

Darby, George (Ed.), *The Times, Past, Present and Future*, Times Publications Ltd, 1985.

Doig, Alan, *Westminster Babylon*, W H Allen, 1990.

Garland, Nicholas, *Not Many Dead*, Hutchinson, 1990.

Glover, Stephen, *Paper Dreams*, Jonathan Cape, 1993.

Hoey, Brian, *The New Royal Court*, Sidgwick and Jackson, 1990.

Leapman, Michael, *Treacherous Estate*, Hodder and Stoughton, 1992.

MacArthur, Brian, Shah, Eddy, *Today and the Newspaper Revolution*, David and Charles, 1988.

McNair, Brian, *News and Radio Journalism in the UK*, Routledge, 1994.

Paletz, David L, Schmid, Alex P, *Terrorism and the Media*, Sage Publications, 1992.

Public Relations Consultants Association, *All You Need To Know About PR*, 1994.

Rosenblum, Mort, *Who Stole the News?*, John Wiley and Sons, 1993.

Sampson, Anthony, *The Essential Anatomy of Britain*, Coronet Books, 1993.

Seymour-Ure, Colin, *The British Press and Broadcasting Since 1945*, Blackwell, 1993.

Shawcross, William, *Rupert Murdoch*, Chatto and Windus, 1992.

Snoddy, Raymond, *The Good, the Bad and the Unacceptable*, Faber and Faber, 1993.

Taylor, S J, *Shock! Horror! The Tabloids in Action*, Bantam Press, 1991.

Index